W9-DBB-764

THE MAN WHO WENT BACK

THE MAN
WHO WENT BACK

by

Lucien Dumais

with Hugh Popham

LEO COOPER · LONDON

First published in Great Britain 1975 by
LEO COOPER LTD,
196 Shaftesbury Avenue, London WC2

Copyright © Lucien Dumais 1975

ISBN 085052 169 6

Printed in Great Britain by
Clarke, Doble and Brendon Ltd
at Plymouth

CONTENTS

ILLUSTRATIONS

The author and publishers would like to thank William H. Spinning for permission to reproduce photographs nos 10, 11, 12, 13, and 15.

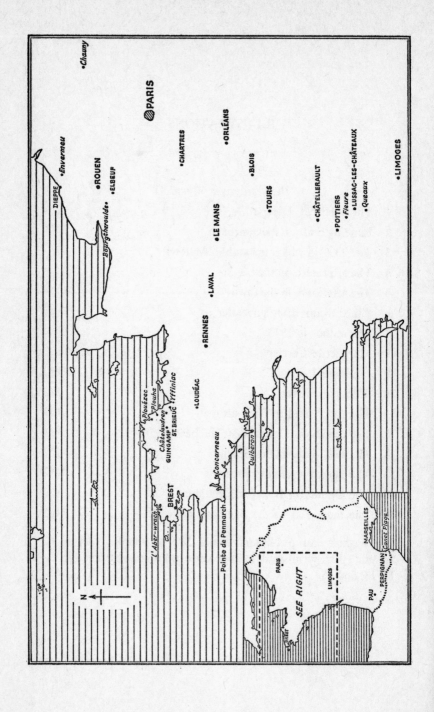

PART ONE

Dieppe, Capture and Escape

On the Way to Dieppe

1

WHEN I woke up it was 0400 and our landing-craft was gliding over a calm sea. The sky was clear and sprinkled with stars that shone like jewels on a background of blue velvet. A very light breeze brought us the coolness and perfume of the sea and the night.

The men were sleeping like children, without a care. As I looked at them before going into action for the first time, I wondered which ones would be killed. In a raid of this sort, even if things went well, we were bound to have casualties; I only hoped they would not be too heavy. Above all, I hoped that every one of us would do his duty to the utmost.

2

Someone was groaning and tossing. It was Private Roberto from my platoon, a sloppy and excitable young man who would never make a good soldier. Next to him was Private Henri Malo, one of the carrier drivers. With his experience he should have been a sergeant by now, but he was not interested in promotion and did not want the responsibility. Then there was Lance Corporal Taylor, a good NCO and a very serious man. He was liked well enough, and managed to get his work done, but off-duty he was inclined to be a loner.

Lance Corporal Vermette had got up and was stretching

3

himself. He was a chubby little man, and a lot of the soldiers called him 'Dad' because he was thirty-five. He had told them to shut up about this as he did not want me to notice his age. He was storeman for our mortar platoon and, being neat and orderly, did a good job. But that was not enough for him and, during our training, although there was no need, he came out on every strenuous route march with his rifle and pack-sack like the rest of the platoon.

I thought, sitting there in that most uncomfortable boat, without room to lie down, that I, the tough old sergeant-major well past thirty-seven years of age, was just a sentimental old fool worrying about my men, who would be most surprised to read my thoughts.

In a few hours we should be landing in France; this arrival would be very different from the arrival I had dreamed of as a young man. Many times I had imagined it all—the planning, the packing, the excitement of life aboard a big passenger ship, and the arrival at docks crowded with people waving a welcome. Then, of course, there would be Paris! We French-speaking Canadians of French descent loved France as the land of our forefathers. In our homes her traditions had been kept alive; some of my earliest memories were of my father singing a rousing Breton song, 'La Paimpolaise', and of my mother rocking us to sleep with 'Fais dodo mon petit gars', an old French lullaby. How many of us would go back to sing those songs to our own children?

3

For we were in the heart of a war; and at that time, in a raiding-craft crossing the Channel, my thoughts roamed back to Canada, my homeland. What had been happening there since we had left two years ago? We had seen a lot of countries in that time—Iceland, Scotland, England, and now France. We had worked hard at being good infantry soldiers and it had not all come easily. We had sweated it out in the heat and we had suffered in the cold. We had been hungry and thirsty and tired, as much as men might be. We had learned to rely on ourselves and on our training.

4

When war was declared the Canadian Army consisted of approximately 4,500 permanent troops. These had to man the general staffs and instructional cadres.

The Royal 22nd Regiment, with about 200 men, was the only French-speaking unit of the permanent force, and the sole source of instructors for the new French-speaking battalions. Consequently the war-time army had to use mainly non-permanent militia, whose members had to recruit and train the new soldiers.

In 1934, when I was twenty-nine years old and supposed to know better, I had joined Les Fusiliers Mont-Royal as a reserve. As far as I knew there had never been any soldiers in my family and they strongly disapproved of such dangerous nonsense. But I had been heading that way since I was ten, when I commanded my younger brother and my sisters in endless war games; later I developed a passion for guns and all violent sports. My small stature gave me, I suppose, something of an inferiority complex; I was touchy, quarrelsome, and determined to excel in all I did. As a result I grew strong and athletic and very gradually learned to control my temper.

Military life suited me down to the ground. Until the war we were part-time volunteers and our maximum training was fifteen days under canvas each summer—if our employers would let us go—with one or two evenings a week during the rest of the year. There was not much encouragement: two tramway tickets, a pack of six cigarettes from one of our officers who manufactured them, a bottle of soda and a plate of beans. The army loaned us the uniform, free of charge, but we had to supply our own boots, shirts and underwear. However I soon found myself looking forward all year to those summer camps, where we handled firearms and lived like real soldiers, and I was very pleased when, in 1937, I was sent to the Military School at Saint-Jean to qualify as a sergeant.

When war broke out everyone, from established NCOs like me to the new civilian entry, had to sign for voluntary service overseas. We drilled our recruits wearing only part of a uniform, sometimes just a cap, with stripes pinned to our civilian coats. For a long time the recruits wore their own clothes; this was a handicap as we could not order them to do anything that would spoil them. We had no equipment, apart from a rifle for every fourth or fifth man, and about ten old, worn-out machine-guns left over from the 1914 war. Six months later, when I was commanding the anti-tank platoon, we not only had no trucks to tow the guns—we had no guns! We learned the mechanics from a handbook, and carried out sham drill in front of a picture of a gun. Nobody in the platoon had ever seen a real one. It was difficult to keep up the men's interest with this sort of thing; they tried hard, though, and took up position around the picture imagining things as best they could. The loading of ammunition was an easy job, since we had none.

Once we reached England things were better. We had mortars and bombs, even if we got very little firing practice. That was being reserved for the enemy. However, when I was sent on a commando instructors' course, it was a different thing altogether.

4

The commandos had unorthodox but efficient ways of using weapons, but as I was champion marksman of my battalion and chief instructor in mortars, I expected to be able to show them a trick or two.

When the 3-inch mortar was brought out, Sergeant Dubuc and I demonstrated how it could be fired by only two men and without sights, bipod or baseplate. This was a good stunt and, although the instructors refused to be impressed, we noticed later that they were secretly practising it.

To cap it they showed us how to fire a rifle from the hip at the speed of a sub-machine-gun, ten rounds in seven seconds. We could hardly believe this until we examined the holes in the target. We asked the instructor to demonstrate again, with another rifle, and we analysed the movement carefully. The first shot went off before the bolt was locked in place, the explosion opened it, and when the bolt was pushed forward the middle finger was held stiff so that it pressed the trigger. Thus, rocking the hand backwards and forwards gave a continuous firing.

Those commandos were not exactly children, though they never succeeded in making us admit it. With a little practice we could soon use our rifles in the same way and became expert in the wastage of ammunition. And to think that, so far, we had been taught that one well-placed bullet was worth ten scattered to the winds!

At the school we learned to do some extraordinary things, some of which were at first sight impossible. The main lesson, we learnt, was that manuals of discipline, training and drill had simply ceased to exist. We were free to do whatever we liked, as long as we accomplished our various tasks in the most efficient way possible. Contrary to regular army practice, all ammunition, including grenades and explosives, was left in an open shed in the middle of the yard and we were invited to help ourselves.

We cut down trees with explosives and blew up rocks, and every crow in the vicinity attracted a fusillade of shots. Soon the environs of the school looked like a battlefield. The CO put up a notice that a sheep had been killed and a cow wounded. It slowed down our activities, but not for long. The madhouse ended, by common consent, only when a student was wounded badly enough to be kept in hospital. Things then became normal again and firing was reserved for the range, with the usual precautions being taken.

It was all part of the course. The commandos held that discipline should be self-imposed, not demanded by superiors; therefore we had to see for ourselves that it was necessary. Obviously, such a demonstration could work only with well-trained soldiers; applied to recruits it would result in massacre!

For my part, I was having a merry old time. Action and adventure had always appealed to me, and the tougher the better. Even the forced marches, designed to test our stamina to the limit, gave me the satisfaction of surviving them at least as well as younger men.

So I was sorry that we could not stay to finish the course. In May, 1942, my battalion was selected to train as commandos, and all its NCOs were recalled. We went with the first-line troops to the Isle of Wight to practise landing exercises.

At this period of the war, the Germans were not getting things all their own way any more. They had been beaten out of the British skies, and there had been successful commando raids on Norway, Bruneval and St Nazaire. The battle of the Atlantic was beginning to turn in our favour and the losses in the convoys were lessening. At last we could afford to remove troops from coastal defence and prepare for attack.

Our training as commandos was designed to transform us from hard and well-disciplined troops into men who refused to give up. Physical and psychological resistance had to be brought to a peak. To this end, we drove our men more and more ruthlessly. We were asking for more than they could give —and we got it—and then we asked for still more.

Our assault course went uphill, naturally; but we made them go over it five or six times until they could not stand up. At that point the officers and NCOs called them lead-swingers, cissies, softies and other fine names, until they pushed forward on all fours and crawled to the assault point and stuck their bayonets into the straw-filled dummies. As long as one man was still able to stand up, we told the others that they should be with him and not letting him down.

We trained in most dangerous conditions, climbing vertical cliffs in the minimum time, and crossing rivers on a rope, after somebody had swum across to fix it. Each man had to get over with his full equipment, and that was where we found out how cumbersome a rifle can be. Jumping into the sea 200 feet off shore, fully dressed and holding our rifles above our heads, was a good way to get drowned. A tall man might have water over his head or up to his knees. One tried to follow in his tracks but it was easy to stumble off the line into deeper water. Some rifles were lost in these mad scrambles.

We found that the sea was always cold, with some seasons colder than others. Uniforms never dried out, and we suffered from chafing under the arms and between the thighs from the wet woollen shirts and heavy trousers. Those who had rejected the army underwear for something more elegant paid for the experience and were soon back in the unglamorous semi-long army issue.

To make things a little more unpleasant, we went moonlight bathing. We jumped into unknown waters at dead of night and found that this was no less cold than day bathing. To warm up we marched fifteen or twenty miles with an extra thirty pounds of ammunition. If we did not suffer from chafing, we were almost certain to blister our feet in the wet boots.

We lived in the open for several weeks with only a ground-sheet, a gas-cape, and two blankets for protection. We slept in our damp uniforms and when it rained we just got a little wetter. When we started work in the morning an orderly, usually a sick man, stayed behind to watch over our things and get them dry if possible. He would build a fire and arrange the spare boots round it; many of them ended up slightly overdone.

There was no question of using blanks for training: when firing around or over our troops we used regular service ammunition. Bullets were one thing—they tend to go where they are aimed—but explosives such as grenades, mortar bombs and shells quite another. One day Captain Larue from our company was wounded in the temple by gravel thrown up from an explosion seventy feet away. On the same day I was the victim of one of our home-made, plastic hand grenades. I was coming out of a building that we used for house-to-house fighting. I heard 'Take cover!' and dived for the ground—but never got there. I was lifted, spun around, and woke up with my head in the corner, stunned, but without a scratch. I carried on my duties but was stone deaf at first.

Having held the battalion championship for rifle shooting, I was often detailed to fire close to our soldiers and scare them if possible, and this was not easy. They knew that we were firing to miss them, and they had faith in our accuracy!

One afternoon the men were made to crawl along a ditch while we fired a bren-gun over them. One soldier refused to get dirty and we could see his kit moving above the top of the trench. Using my very accurate rifle, I put a bullet right through his haversack less than two inches from his skin. His water bottle was pierced, and as the tepid water ran down his back he subsided quickly in the mud, convinced he had been hit.

9

It may seem cruel to scare men like this but it is the proper way to train them: make them believe they are in danger of being killed and keep them advancing as ordered. To reach this degree of discipline, we prepared a special assault course that the soldiers had to cross at a run. It was strewn with explosive charges that went off while they were crossing it, and we warned them to watch the ground ahead of them for mines. Explosions took place between them and around them; the NCOs had quite a job getting the men to go across. What they did not know was that the charges were controlled from a nearby hut and were fired only when we were sure that nobody stood close enough to get hurt. This had to be given up when a soldier walked slowly into the supposed minefield, stopped and lit a cigarette. Charges close to him were exploded, but he refused to move; it was his way of telling us that he was not going to be fooled any longer.

The most dangerous training of all was 'house clearing', which we practised in bombed houses that had been evacuated. The instructors had gone round beforehand filling them with booby traps. Live grenades might land at our feet when we opened a door, or realistically-armed dummies wait for us in a closet. We had to learn to react quickly and correctly to all manner of surprises.

6

In June we carried out our first practice landing, near Bridport. The higher authorities were not satisfied. Too many things went wrong: we embarked in the wrong ships, arrived late on the beaches, and were not put ashore at the exact spot. A repeat was ordered.

This took place on 22 June and was not nearly so funny. The defending British troops had got hold of some ammunition and fired a few rounds just over our heads. All the carts we had used before to transport our mortars had been immobilized with chains, and when the re-embarkation was due, the platoon from 'C' Company that covered our withdrawal could hardly extricate itself. The officer in charge ordered smoke-bombs from his two-inch mortar, but the defending troops just marched through the smoke to pester him a bit more. It took a round of HE before he got room in which to operate.

For this second practice we used commando raiding-craft. These were half-decked plywood boats, twenty-five feet long by six feet wide, painted white, and powered by twin Ford engines. The crew consisted of one officer and two sailors, and each boat carried twenty soldiers and their equipment. These craft were fast and manœuvrable. They could come right to the shoreline, as they drew little water and were very silent at slow speed. A tarpaulin supported on hoops, and a large windshield forward gave some protection from the weather, but there was no protection whatever from enemy fire.

7

This was the type of craft we were in now, on our way to Dieppe. It was not the first time. Once before, early in July, we had embarked for the real thing, but after five days of waiting it had been cancelled owing to bad weather. That morning, 19 August, the sea was like glass, and we were already half-way there.

Although we NCOs had been given no opportunity to study the plans, I had managed to find out quite a lot. Two groups of British commandos were to land first and knock out two gun batteries, one at Bruneval, east of Dieppe, and the other at Varengeville, to the west. This was instead of using parachutists and heavy bombardment by naval guns, which had been part of the previous plan. The German batteries were powerful and had to be destroyed if we were to be able to land. We fervently hoped that the commandos would be successful.

The 4th and 6th Canadian Brigades were to be supported by the 14th Armoured Regiment and quite a number of detachments from the Signals, Engineers, Artillery, etc. There were 6,000 men engaged in this raid, not including the Navy and the Air Force. Some of the Air Force would be American bombers. From the numbers involved I gathered that it was going to be quite a performance.

According to advance information the enemy were not particularly strong at Dieppe and, although they had some defences, they were not too extensive. There had been no indications that we were expected, and we badly needed the element of surprise. A forewarned enemy would be much stronger than we were, even with our numbers and all our weapons.

Our battalion had been designated as a floating reserve, to be thrown into any breach made in the enemy defences. As we were embarked in unarmoured ships, we were to land only on already occupied ground, well defended by our first wave of troops.

CHAPTER TWO

The Raid

1

ON the sea it was too dark to see much: a few of the 'R Craft' of our own little flotilla but nothing else. We could hear nothing either, except the throaty sound of our own motors, as we moved ahead at half speed. In a few hours we should be meeting the enemy, so we had none too much time to go through the whole plan, in so far as it concerned us, and check that everything was ready.

The men were waking up now, and climbing to the narrow side decks, which were about twenty-four inches wide and just right to sit on. Sergeant Brunet was also awake and rattling on with his usual string of jokes at other people's expense. At that precise minute he was attacking Private Goyette on the state of his weapons. For Goyette, who looked after his machine-gun as if it were a rare Stradivarius and did not allow anyone to touch it, such kidding from a superior was not funny. He would have liked to make some retort that would shut the sergeant up, but he was not the man to do it. He was a rather ingenuous country boy, slow in thought and speech, and certainly no match for the sergeant, who was a bit of a city slicker.

The eastern sky was beginning to lighten. Dawn was coming up, a brilliant pink, and a slight haze rose from the sea, the prelude to a fine summer's day. Wherever we looked now, there were ships; the Channel seemed full of ALCs, fat troop transports, sleek destroyers bristling with guns, TLCs: a vast flotilla. All was calm and undisturbed, like some great peacetime review.

Suddenly there was a noise in the far distance. We listened intently. It was too early for the assault. The naval officer cut the speed and our boat settled in the water. We all held our breath in an attempt to catch the least sound, but all we could hear was the gentle slapping of the waves against the side of the boat. Then, from astern, came two short blasts on a siren, and a destroyer emerged from the light fog only to rush past, full of majesty and chasing with its bow a mass of white foam as flimsy as a bridal veil.

Then we heard the first shots of the raid; who fired them we could not tell.* This was the first time any of us had been under fire and we all ducked We awaited the arrival of the shells—twenty, twenty-five, thirty seconds, they were not for us. But in no time at all we too should have to be reaching for our steel helmets.

I pulled myself together and began to get everyone busy. We had to shave and wash in sea water; I tried to convince the men that sea water was very good for the gums! In the best tradition, we could not die without a shave and shiny boots. Nobody had a brush, so we had to borrow a rag from one of the sailors.

We had a little food with us, but not nearly enough. I was lucky enough to find some extra emergency rations, and I shared these out. We had never tasted them before, although all of us had been carrying some in our bags. They come in a tin just like sardines, with a key to roll back the cover. Inside was a sort of chocolate marked off in squares. Its taste was very pleasant, just like chocolate, and I was sorry we had so little as there was not going to be enough to go round. It was not long before I discovered my mistake; it was as much as I could do to eat a second square. We all had more than we could eat, and no one would die hungry.

A destroyer on our right suddenly opened up with its heavy guns; we felt at last that that pleasant sea voyage of ours had come to an end. The dreamy haze of that August morning had been finally and firmly dispelled; the fighting we had been preparing for for three years was on us. It was the

* In fact it was the unlucky chance encounter with a German escorted convoy that lost us the priceless advantage of surprise.

first time that Canadian troops had been in action in the war. It would be the first time the name of our regiment was mentioned in a battle, and we had to uphold the tradition that the veterans of the last war had handed down to us. They were known to be men of valour, and in France their names were synonymous with heroism.

From our rear, we could hear the sound of aircraft: the Allies coming from England. As they passed overhead, we could see they were fighters making for Dieppe. There were quite a few of them and our men cheered.

Our landing-craft had slowed down again and we were barely moving. Now we could hear the roar of guns from the sea: there was a steady firing from the ships near us, pouring shells into Dieppe. So far, none had come our way in reply. We had no means of knowing what was going on; the early morning haze had become thicker with the gun smoke, and judging by the sound of exploding shells, we were too far from land to see anything anyway.

Next, waves of light bombers came roaring in from the sea. This was just about the time the first Canadian landing was due. The British should have landed about an hour previously, and if things had gone well for them, their job should be almost finished.

On our right flank, the South Saskatchewan should have been attacking Pourville, and on our left the Royal Regiment of Canada should have been attacking Puys. I explained to the men what I knew of the plan and what should have been happening. Their nerves were calmed; somebody had produced a pack of tattered cards, and they were soon at their favourite pastime. I think that if they had to wait at the gates of hell, they would sit down and start shuffling.

So far the aircraft had all been ours. Now suddenly a Focke Wulf appeared from nowhere, making straight for us. All the ships in the vicinity engaged it at once, and the soldiers from our flotilla opened up with rifles, sten- and bren-guns. It twisted away in a half roll, black smoke trailing from its engine. We could see the pilot struggling to get out of his cockpit, but it was too late: the plane dived into the sea. This was our first encounter with the enemy.

Just about then, if everything had gone according to schedule, the second wave should have been landing. The Royal Hamilton Light Infantry should have been moving in on White Beach, just below the Casino; the Essex Scottish should have been landing on Red Beach, to the left, close to the harbour, and the Queen's Own Highlanders of Canada were due to land behind the SSR, and push through to meet the tanks, which by then should have made a breach and gone round to their rendezvous at the airport, south of Dieppe.

Quite suddenly, we emerged from the fog and smoke into a bright, strange and sunny world. Some destroyers were firing for all they were worth; the noise was quite deafening. There must have been over 250 ships, and the Channel seemed crowded with them. We had picked up speed and were getting rapidly closer. As the smoke cleared, we could see Dieppe. Some landing-craft were coming away from the shore and they were being fired on. Shells were bursting between them, they fanned out, and the big guns gave them covering fire.

However, something had gone wrong, because not all the enemy guns had been put out of action yet. If the boats were being fired at as they came out, we should get the same treatment as we went in. But for the moment we were out of range, and did not need to go in at all.

On our right a destroyer opened fire. It was shooting at the cliff to the right of Dieppe, where an answering flash showed that there was a gun sited in a cottage or blockhouse. The shell was aimed at the destroyer, but it missed and a jet of water shot up very near us. We were about 200 yards from the destroyer and we sheered off a little, but we could not do much to keep out of trouble in such a press of boats, and on the other side of us there was another destroyer also being fired at.

The first destroyer let off a salvo which seemed to land to the left of the blockhouse. A second salvo went to the right but closer; a third was bang on target, and the blockhouse disappeared in a cloud of smoke. My men were showing the greatest interest all this time—and betting on the results. When the target was hit a loud cheer went up for the gun crew. An officer on the deck of the destroyer leant over and waved to us, evidently meaning 'Thanks'.

Suddenly another destroyer came streaking out of the haze and smoke, making straight for us. Our landing-craft shook as the stern was thrown hard round; but the destroyer went past, missing us by a hair's breadth. We breathed again; it had been a close one. If we were going to die, we would just as soon do a little fighting first.

The smoke round Dieppe was clearing, and with my binoculars I tried to make out what was going on. On our right flank, I could see an open beach with some houses at the far end. This must have been Pourville where the SSR were supposed to have landed, followed by the Queen's Own. To the left of the open beach there was quite a cliff, perhaps half a mile long, and as white as the cliffs of Dover. On top of them I could see occasional puffs of smoke. Then to the left again, the cliffs sloped down to Dieppe beach; I could see the old castle and a building on the beach itself, which must have been the Casino. Behind that there was the steeple of St Rémy Church, but I could not make it out very well at that distance.

Dieppe beach extended for about a mile, and then there was the harbour with rocky cliffs both behind it and beyond it on the extreme left. Intelligence reported that there were guns and machine-guns on the cliffs to our right, in the harbour, and also on the high ground to the left of the harbour; and machine-guns all along the esplanade and in the hotels facing it. The Casino was heavily defended, and there were some medium guns at Puys, but they should have been put out of action by now.

I wondered if the tanks had landed successfully with the second wave. The enemy should have been quite surprised, as this was the first time tanks of this size had been landed so close behind the infantry. We hoped that the troops of the first and second waves had got ashore before dawn; the beach seemed to be under heavy fire, and it would be suicidal to land in broad daylight. We would need more than a smoke screen to keep the casualties down. Heavy guns in close support would be essential.

We knew that the beach was a minimum of 200 yards wide

at high tide; at the top of the beach, blocking it off, were rows of strong top-quality concertina wire. We should have to get through this, but the preceding troops were supposed to have blasted a way through with Bangalore torpedoes. Beyond the wire, a continuous wall had been formed by joining the hotel walls and closing the streets with concrete slabs eight feet high.

I wished I had a radio to find out what was happening, but only the platoon commander had one; our little ship had to play follow-my-leader and use hand signals.

Overhead the RAF did not seem very busy, although we could see some fighting in the distance.

We had been advancing all this time but now the flotilla put on more speed. This was it, we were going in!

2

'All right everybody, blow your Mae Wests up now, get your equipment on and load your weapons.'

An MTB came up from the stern at some speed, the CO on its foredeck. He addressed us with a megaphone.

'I've just had new orders from General Roberts. We're to land in the centre of Dieppe beach. I expect you all to do your job. We'll show 'em what we're made of! The mortars will engage the heights on the right. Good luck, boys!'

He went round the flotilla, repeating his message. The MTB then sped ahead to catch up with the CO's R-craft. He climbed down into it, and prepared to lead his battalion into attack. He wanted to be the first to land.

We increased speed, and some shells started to come our way. With my glasses I could see a grounded and burning tank-landing craft below the Casino. Then aircraft flew low over the esplanade and began to lay a heavy smoke screen; it began drifting slowly seaward.

It was now 0700 hours, and we were going on to White Beach, right behind the RHLI. Although the shelling was not too serious, through a rift in the smoke-screen I could see that our troops were still fighting on the beach and that our tanks were firing. The enemy had not been put out of action and as we were going in without armour we had to expect heavy casualties. My platoon was going to have a tough job, as it would take us a full minute to unload our mortar material.

It was time to get ready. Private Goyette came up on to the small foredeck with his bren-gun and lay down in a firing position to starboard, and the gunner from the pioneer platoon did the same on the other side. I took my place behind Goyette, as I was to be the second man ashore; a bomb carrier was passed up to me from the hold. There was a rift in the smoke-screen ahead and as the tops of the buildings came into sight I shouted an order to the two bren-gunners.

'Open fire on those windows you see through the smoke, range 800.'

At that distance the firing could not be expected to be very effective, but I wanted to show the men we were going in to fight.

But soon I noticed that with the slight pitching of the boat the guns were pointing just about everywhere, and as we probably had men on the beach, we might well shoot them in the back. I called out to the gunners:

'Cease fire! '

That was the first time I had ordered my men to fire at an enemy, and it was not a success.

About a hundred yards from the smoke screen, our flotilla put on full speed. Then all hell broke loose. The pall of smoke became a tornado of fire and steel. Every enemy gun must have been trained on it, and it seemed crazy to go in. The smoke was being twisted into a variety of shapes by the exploding shells and bombs. There was a continuous roar, unbroken even for the fraction of a second.

Just before we got to the screen, a sheer wall of water rose in front of us. It must have been thirty feet high, and it dared us to cross it. The CO's R-craft went into the smoke; he was still in the lead, but I wondered how long he would last. Then tracer bullets began to come through in a criss-cross pattern.

We had so far managed to keep our formation: the CO's boat and then four abreast, six deep, well lined up, as if we were on parade. It was a grand sight, this deployment of little white skiffs. The enemy would hardly imagine we should keep going

19

in the face of such a barrage; but now that we had shown our intentions, and were coming within their reach, they were out to tear us apart. The smoke screen was a flaming vortex. Behind us we could hear our heavy guns firing for all they were worth.

All we could see then was the sky, and that, too, was chaotic as aircraft churned and fired at one another. The ack-ack guns were adding to the turmoil with shells that soared skyward and exploded into black puffs of smoke. Several planes came spinning down, looking like great wounded birds in their death-throes, diving into the green sea and quenching their fierceness.

A mortar bomb hit the water on our port side and I could hear the shrapnel whistling. There appeared to be no damage, in spite of our lack of protection. I called out:

'Everybody O.K. below?'

Sergeant Brunet answered:

'Everybody intact.'

Another bomb fell ahead, and a piece of shrapnel came through the windshield, nothing else. We had been lucky—so far! Another bomb landed astern and another to starboard. This time several splinters ripped through the panelling, and the explosion knocked our boat off course. The officer at the helm brought it back into line. A corporal called out from below:

'Two wounded this time, Sergeant Brunet and Lance Corporal Taylor.'

Sergeant Brunet's face was covered in blood, and a soldier was applying a dressing to Taylor's shoulder; they had both picked up a piece of shrapnel. It was no use landing them: we needed able-bodied men ashore; so I yelled out above the noise:

'The wounded will remain on board under the care of the crew. Lay them down below water level; all others be ready to land.'

In actual fact, Brunet's wound was only a deep scratch under the nose, nothing too serious, but when he felt the burn, he had passed his hand over the wound and smeared himself with blood, so he looked worse than he was. He would find this out in a few moments, no doubt and go ashore with the others.

Two more bombs exploded very near us, and a burst of machine-gun fire whistled past our heads; instinctively I ducked. This first time under fire, with the enemy throwing everything at us, I had a very curious feeling of self-pity. I began to think the enemy was definitely unreasonable to be doing this to me, it was very dangerous and he might kill me. One's normal sense of being under the protection of the law was suddenly withdrawn, and left one feeling terribly vulnerable.

Everybody made himself as small as possible and that included me. I was in my position on deck and very exposed; I should have much preferred to have been with the men down in the boat and below the waterline. For a man who had crossed the Atlantic just to fight the enemy, this seemed a curious reaction. I had to remind myself that I was supposed to be a tough sergeant-major of the crack 2nd Division.

We were in the smoke screen for less than a minute, as we were travelling at full speed. It seemed risky to carry on at this rate as we were ignorant of the distance to the shore and might have run aground, but that was the naval officer's responsibility, and I put it out of my mind.

The smoke cleared a bit; the CO's boat ahead appeared to be down by the stern, but I quickly realized that this was because of the speed. The CO was crouching on deck ready to jump ashore. We must have been doing over twenty-five knots, and a lot of explosions could be seen between the ships. An R-craft on our right was hit on its fore-deck on the port side. It swerved, but came back into line and kept its speed up. They must have had pretty heavy casualties on board, but the boat kept on heading for the beach.

Further to the right, another boat came out of the smoke and I recognized Sergeant-Major Hogues from 'A' Coy; he was known as 'Popeye' because of his cracked voice. His boat had veered to starboard and was making for the cliff. Suddenly there was a burst of machine-gun fire, he straightened up from his half-bent position, let go of the handrail, and pitched into the sea. There went an old friend; we first met in 1934. He must have been one of the first in the battalion to be killed; his fight had not been a long one, he had probably not even seen the enemy.

Below the Casino at the top of the beach, there was a grounded TLC. It lay broadside on to the shore and over its open ramp I could see that the tanks had been landed. It was burning furiously aft and the ammunition stowed there was exploding, fanning the flames into an inferno.

Red tracer bullets were coming at us from a hotel straight in front, and I told the gunners to engage that target as soon as they had landed.

The beach was a shambles, and a lot of our men from the second wave were lying there either wounded or dead. Some of the wounded were swimming out to meet our flotilla and the sea was red with their blood. Some sank and disappeared. We stood by as they died, powerless to help: we were there to fight, not to pick up the drowning and the wounded. But the whole operation was beginning to look like a disaster.

3

The officer brought our vessel to a halt at the water's edge. The two gunners jumped off, ran up the beach, threw themselves down, and opened fire on the hotel windows. I jumped down on to the beach right behind Goyette. I was still carrying last night's heavy load of ammunition I had picked up and the thirty-pound mortar-bomb carrier; I dumped the carrier and turned to take more from the man behind me.

The boat had started to back away. I signalled the officer to come forward, but he continued to reverse and some of the men started jumping into the water. One of my corporals was yelling at him to stay near the beach.

The skipper took no notice. It looked as if he was scared stiff, and was not going to wait for us to disembark our mortar. I pulled my pistol out and threatened to shoot him, but he ducked below the foredeck out of sight.* The boat backed away faster, and the men from both platoons jumped into the sea which was now shoulder deep. All of them had their rifles; good

* This is how it looked to me from the beach: in fact, as Sergeant Brunet saw, the skipper had been killed by a German bullet.

for them! The many lessons had borne fruit, they were still a fighting force.

All this time, the inferno had, if anything been getting worse. More machine-guns were firing at us now that they could see their target. Standing up on the beach, my back turned to the enemy, yelling and waving orders and acting like a commander, I was surprised not to have been killed already.

I threw myself to the ground and signalled the men to do the same. I had to consider the best course of action. The landing-craft had gone, and with it our mortars and most of our bombs. There was no hope of getting any more. So we should have to fight as riflemen. I motioned to the men to open out. It was no use yelling; they would not have heard me.

Many of the RHLI had been cut down on the beach. It was now the FMRs who were falling right and left. The enemy fire was murderous; there was not only shrapnel from the mortars but shingle thrown up by the explosions. Tracer bullets were cutting the air in every direction, especially across our front. Most of them came from our flanks, and as for every tracer there were four invisible bullets, the air was seething with flying steel.

The whole thing was like being in the middle of a very busy intersection with traffic from four directions at once, and it made one dizzy. It seemed impossible to make the 200 yards of beach without being killed. Nobody could get through that.

Yet we could not stay on the beach in the open, in full view of the enemy. It was only a matter of time before they killed every one of us. The nearest cover was the Casino; so we had to make for that and take it over. It was some thirty-five feet to my right. I got up, and half crouching, moved ten or twelve feet towards it, signalling the men to follow me. Some of them got ready, and I moved over again to the right. When I dropped to the ground, I tried to give the impression I had been hit.

Four or five feet away and slightly higher up on the beach lay Lieutenant Pierre Loranger, my platoon commander, with his batman applying a field dressing to his thighs. Loranger signalled me to come to him, and he told me that with wounds in both thighs he was unable to carry on, and that I was to take over the platoon. He gave me his map and a sten-gun he had been carrying as an extra weapon. I wished him good luck and started moving towards the Casino again.

I still had the bombs, but they would not have been of any use, so I threw them away. I tried to slip the map into my blouse, but the Mae West was still inflated: I let the air out of it and breathing became immediately easier.

I made a short dash up and to the right, towards a blockhouse standing in front of the Casino. Several of our tanks were moving about, trying to get on to the esplanade; one had a broken track, but all were firing like mad with their guns and machine-guns. Well, if the infantry could not do much, at least the tanks were giving the Germans hell whenever they could pinpoint their positions.

It was impossible to say exactly where the enemy fire was coming from; the tracers seemed to originate in mid-air. But my reaction as a trained soldier was to move forward fast; a burst of machine-gun fire arrived just where I had been lying. I was up and away again, and another burst arrived, just missing me. The gunner, I reckoned, was in a window of the third floor right in front, and I put a mental X on it.

My jump had brought me behind one of our tanks, and for the moment at least I was partly protected. Some of my men had come up a little way; others seemed to have been hit. I could not go back and look after them; I had to get forward and under cover to reorganize whatever troops we had left. From the number of wounded and dead lying about, there would not be many left for fighting.

I felt a severe blow on my steel helmet, and on examining it found it had a large dent in it, probably from a flying rock. A moment later a chunk half the size of my fist thumped my left arm and went bouncing away. This was mortar work; the air was full not only of shrapnel but also of flying splinters of rock. So far I had been lucky.

Since seeing the boat pull away, I had been fighting mad; and now my fury increased. Very soon somebody was going to pay for all this.

A soldier came from the beach on my right, and threw himself down behind the tracks of the tank. As if on a signal the tank backed up and crushed him. In front of the tank a soldier got up suddenly—just as the tank opened fire with its machine-gun. The soldier's headless body fell back to the ground. Tanks give good protection, but the crew cannot see anybody close up. This was worth remembering.

I jumped up and ran to the blockhouse; no fire was coming from it. Round the back, the door was half open and I looked inside, ready to throw a grenade if anything moved. A German corporal was lying dead. He was the first enemy soldier I had seen. He was wearing his gas-mask; he must have thought that the smoke screen contained gas. The blockhouse had been cleaned out by men of the RHLI.

Between the blockhouse and the Casino lay numerous dead and wounded; some were groaning, others screaming in anguish, their bodies torn to shreds, dark red blood gushing from terrible wounds. Amongst them were some Germans. This must have been a tough fight for the RHLI; they captured the position but paid heavily for it in the process.

The open space towards the Casino was being swept by tracer from both sides. There was a tangle of barbed wire that had been cut. I made a dash for it, and got through a gap in the wire. Behind me there was a barrage of shots. The Germans had seen me crossing but they reacted too late.

The corner of the Casino formed a redoubt, and this had been turned into a gun position, with sandbags about waist high to seaward. I made for this with my sten-gun at the ready. I jumped over the sandbags and landed right in the midst of soldiers of the RHLI. Protected by the wall of the Casino I turned towards the beach and signalled to my men to come up. Lance Corporal Vermette was coming at the double, accompanied by spurts of machine-gun fire. This must have been the same gunner as was after me, and I intended to get him.

As I knelt behind the sandbags on the left side of the little square and examined the hotel front, there was a sharp pull on my right wrist which brought me to the ground. It was a corporal of the RHLI, and he shouted,

'Sergeant-Major, get down! There's a gunner across the esplanade and he's hit several of the boys and me as well.'

I ignored him and stuck my head up again. Immediately

B

the bullets started whistling and my steel helmet was knocked down over my eyes. There was a burning sensation on the top of my right ear; my steel helmet had something of a bend in the brim. He had put a burst on a level with my eyes, with a bullet on each side of my head. It could hardly have been closer. This time I was livid, not scared, just plain mad. The corporal had a bren-gun across his knees.

'Is this thing working?'

'Yes, sir, but don't get yourself killed. That guy is good.'

'So am I.'

I slapped on a fresh magazine, adjusted the drum, cocked the gun and rested the muzzle on top of the sandbags. I aligned the sights high up the building just about where the gunner should have been. I quickly raised myself and the window was right in my sight, the trigger already down and bullets speeding into the window. Some sprayed the edges of the stone and chips started flying; there would be plenty of dust in that room. I poured a whole magazine of twenty rounds into that window.

I dropped to the ground again and put on a fresh magazine. I lay there, catching my breath and sweating heavily, for a full minute, to let the enemy think that I had moved on.

I bobbed up again suddenly and sprayed the window. This time, though, I fired bursts of five, and each time I took a good look. I thought I could see the muzzle of a gun, but was not sure as there was a lot of dust and smoke.

On the third inspection I could definitely see the muzzle of a gun, and it was pointing upwards, which meant that the butt was on the floor. Either I had knocked out the gunner or he had abandoned his gun. I fired until it fell over.

This was the first time I had fired at an enemy soldier; I hoped I had convinced him that we too could shoot on target.

As I handed the corporal back his bren-gun I could see three German soldiers standing at the corner of the wall. Startled, I reached for my pistol, but a warning voice said:

'Take it easy, Sergeant-Major, everything is under control.'

The speaker, a lieutenant of the RHLI, was sitting down with his back to the wall. He was wounded in the shoulder and leg. Automatically I came to attention and saluted him. He told me to skip the etiquette, and it is true that this was no place for decorum. He said:

'I'm in charge here. We're all wounded and looking after the prisoners.'

He had a sten-gun across his knees and his pistol in his hand.

Vermette came up over the sandbags, he was not wounded but, like me, just out of breath. He was carrying a bren-gun, and reported:

'Some of our men on the beach are too scared to move.'

Corporal Lebel, known as 'Lefty', from my platoon, also arrived from the beach. He had not been in my boat, and he told us that there had been a lot of men wounded on board their boat. He had seen me firing at the enemy gunner and was convinced I had got him.

A stretcher-bearer was giving first aid to a soldier of the RHLI whose arm had been almost torn off at the shoulder. The soldier was bleeding badly; he had not got much chance of coming through alive.

Now that there were three of us, we could try and do something about knocking out some of the enemy. I told the two corporals to investigate inside the Casino while I took a look on the west side. I followed a solarium wall towards the sea, and just before I came to the corner, a German steel helmet appeared about knee high. It was a soldier coming along on all fours. He saw me and tried to raise his sub-machine-gun in his right hand. My sten was in my left hand, but automatically I drew my pistol and fired—first. He collapsed, and his feet beat the ground in a rapid tattoo. I kept my gun in my hand, ready to fire again, but it was not necessary; there was a small hole in his helmet and blood was running down his forehead.

'Two-gun Dumais' had killed his first enemy, at least as a certainty; this one I could see. He was lying there in front of me, his face in the sand, motionless. He was still clutching his gun and I kicked it away, just to make sure that if he was playing dead he would not shoot me in the back.

What was my reaction after this first killing? Pity? Remorse? No, neither. It was a purely professional indifference. I drew faster than he did, so I was alive and he was dead. He should

27

have held his weapon in his left hand and looked round the corner with only his left eye showing. But I should have had my weapon cocked: I was not expecting to meet him any more than he was expecting me. It was only constant pistol practice, that single movement, firing as you drew, that saved me.

The west side of the Casino lay open and was well covered by enemy fire coming from the cliff in front of the old castle. Some of our soldiers were lying there either dead or wounded. An occasional puff of black smoke showed where there was mortar fire. Two German bodies were also out there; they had not had everything their own way.

On the beach below the Casino some of our troops were fighting back. They would soon be as dead as their comrades if they stayed exposed to fire from a hidden enemy. I waved at them, telling them to come to the Casino for cover.

Making my way back to the wounded lieutenant, I asked him just how far their troops had gone. He said they were still fighting in the Casino. Climbing in through a low window in the solarium, I found myself in a small room with a door on the south side. I opened this cautiously with a grenade at the ready. One of our soldiers was guarding two prisoners. I ordered him to turn his prisoners over to the wounded lieutenant and come back to me on the south side. We badly needed the few able-bodied fighting men that remained.

I pressed on into a big room which looked like some sort of guardroom, the floor littered with soldiers' equipment, clothes and boots. There might have been something of military interest, but this was hardly the moment to sort it out. In a large hall beyond, a number of our soldiers were in firing positions at the windows. As machine-gun fire was coming in through the big bay windows, from across the street and from the cliff, the only way to get across the room was to crouch under the window sills. The floor was covered with broken glass, ripped wood and shattered plaster, the dust thick and choking. Corporal Vermette was there, and I told him to engage the top of the cliff, where there seemed to be machine-guns.

Corporal Lebel, accompanied by an FMR soldier, returned from the other side of the main staircase and reported that some Germans had locked themselves up in a sort of blockhouse in the northwest corner of the building. I told him I would deal with them while he went upstairs to see whether it was clear of the enemy. I warned him to be careful, and to look out for our own soldiers as well as Germans.

The corner blockhouse had been built by adding a wall on the inside and a false roof, the entrance being closed by a steel door locked from inside. There must have been firing slits in the outer wall. For the moment there was no sound of firing; but as they could rake the beach at close range it was essential to get them out. It was difficult to see how, as grenades would do more damage to us than them; but they must be put out of action somehow. Through a window on the left side I could see some German soldiers about 150 yards away, on the first floor of a house. There was a cut corner with a door leading on to a small balcony, on which they had mounted a machine-gun. Two were halfway out of the double door and firing down at our men on the beach, while a third was standing back and directing the shooting. They were hardly visible from the beach, but to me they were in full view.

I rested my sten-gun across the window sill, which was about shoulder high, and fired a burst. Nothing happened; they kept on firing. Probably my bullets were going too low, the range being long for a sten. Aiming higher, I fired again. The gun jammed. I cleared it and tried again. It fired three rounds and jammed again. I was disgusted with it and broke it against the wall. I ran back to the top of the beach to pick up a rifle that I had seen abandoned there. It was in good order. On my way back to the west window, I picked up some of our grenades that were lying on the floor.

The three Germans were still there absorbed in firing on the beach. Taking careful aim at the man standing up, who was probably an NCO, I gently pressed the trigger. As the rifle went off, I stepped back and could see my target being thrown backwards, while the other two had dropped flat in the doorway. The gun was still on the little balcony, and I was sure they did not know where my shot had come from.

After a long pause, two eyes appeared in the light of the doorway; they were looking in my direction, but I doubted whether they could see me as I was well back in the shadow and there was a lot of dust in the Casino. With a strange rifle, I did not care to risk this very small target; I would wait, and I was rewarded. The two men returned to their gun, but I did not give them a chance to fire. A second shot was away, and a gunner was hit and pulled inside by his comrade.

I waited a short while to see if the third man would try and be as foolish again. Then there was a sudden explosion, and I found myself on the floor about five feet from the window, with nothing visible for the dust. When I had fully come to I focused on a large hole slightly to the right of where I had been standing. The gunners in the house must have registered my presence at the window and a shot from an anti-tank gun had sent me flying. But there was no machine-gun on the balcony any more.

Going back towards the big hall, I met a sergeant from the Engineers and asked him what he could do with the steel door. He told me he had lots of explosives and would deal with it. There was a large steel handle on the outside, and he fastened some explosives to it. In the meantime I went to the window for a breath of fresh air and to see if anything was happening. There was another terrible blast and I picked myself up from under the window having been almost thrown out of it by the sergeant's charge. He fired it without any warning, probably thinking I had gone to hide round a corner. This time I really could not see straight, and I had difficulty in finding my way in the dust-cloud.

While I paused to catch my breath at the window, wondering whether I was still in one piece, there was a movement on the roof of the blockhouse: somebody was up there; as it could not be any of our men, I called out:

'Kommen Sie unter!'

It may not have been good German, but it brought results. Two of the enemy appeared, hands above their heads, and decidedly shaken. Having signalled them down, I started them on their way to the wounded lieutenant. As the steel door now had a large hole in it, about twelve by eighteen inches, I threw in a couple of grenades. Once again there was nothing to be seen for dust. I was glad to get away from there with my two prisoners.

After handing them over, I went upstairs and found an FMR sergeant with two of his men and two RHLI men engaging the enemy across the street with three bren-guns and their rifles. I sent for Corporal Lebel, and when he had come down with his two men posted him to the defence of the south side with the sergeant. I told them to do their best to counteract the enemy fire and give us cover, while I tried to organize a push into the city. From the first floor they could fire over the anti-tank wall into the Rue de Sygogne, which was the one we were going to use.

I looked round for more men but could find only seriously wounded ones, apart, of course, from the many dead lying around. I had to get things organized into some sort of defence if we were to be of any use, so I went down to the beach, almost to the water's edge, searching for more fit men. I did this at a gallop, periodically throwing myself on the ground. I yelled at everyone in sight to come up to the Casino and get out of the enemy fire. A number of wounded had dragged themselves behind the burning TLC. There were some unhurt soldiers there too, and I told them to come out and do some fighting. Then I made a run for the Casino, with half the German army firing at me, but they were too slow and I was not hit.

A few men made a dash for it, one after another, and most of them got through. A private from my battalion, a very young fellow, jumped in over the sandbags and lay there crying his heart out, just about uncontrollable with fear; I could hardly blame him. Still, I had to get on with my job, and I asked the wounded Lieutenant to see whether he could sort him out. The lieutenant said he would look after him.

How any of us got across that beach alive is more than I shall ever understand. It shows, I suppose, that a running man is not easy to stop.

By now I was very tired, partly because of the full load on my back, but I did not dare drop it, as I was sure to need it if I did.

On the south side of the Casino there was a trench leading off to a shed some forty feet away on the esplanade. Every few feet there was a dead German. Apparently they had been engaged by one of our tanks from the east side and blown up with hand grenades thrown from the windows.

This must be RHLI work. They had done some heavy fighting, more than we had, but then they had landed in the dark, from armoured craft, and protected by tanks. We had had no protection whatever, and the slaughter of our battalion started half a mile from shore. It was surprising that we had got even this far.

In the shed were some ten soldiers of the RHLI, commanded by a lieutenant who was trying to get in touch with his HQ by radio, but without success. He told me that these were the survivors of his company's attack, and probably the only invading troops this high up on the esplanade. The Essex Scottish at the other end of the beach may not have fared as well, as they had had no cover and yet had to cope with the same enemy fire. I asked him to contact my battalion through the Brigade, if he could, and report that we were here and that the Casino had been taken, while I tried to push on into the city proper with the eight men I had with me. I told him about the covering fire from the windows of the Casino. He said his men would help all they could.

A sergeant warned me that firing was coming from an air raid shelter on the boulevard. I was at a loss to know how to stop it, but a tank solved my problem: it had seen the firing and engaged the position with cannon and machine-gun. The enemy fire stopped immediately.

From the corner of the shed, running eastward, there was a low cement wall supporting a heavy grille about six feet high and bordering the esplanade. Thick bushes lined the wall on the seaward side, and we would have protection from assault, fire and view, so we took cover among the bushes.

One of our tanks climbed up from the beach at the end of the grille about 150 yards away. It rolled on to the esplanade with its gun pointing towards the old castle, the direction from which it seemed to be expecting trouble. An enemy gun fired at it from the harbour, hitting it on the left side, to the back of the turret. The tank stopped. I thought to myself, there goes another big fighter, one we needed badly. But no, its periscope turned towards the enemy gun. But another shot hit it in the same spot; this must be it. Then a third shot, in the same place, a completely one-sided duel. It made me mad to see one of our tanks knocked out so easily at a crucial moment like that.

But—what was this? The tank-cannon was moving round through 180° and fast too. It was hardly on target when three shots rang out in quick succession. WOOF! WOOF! WOOF! The tank was not dead by a long chalk, and was shooting fast and furiously.

The tank stood there, waiting for a reply, and it seemed to be asking how's it feel to get a dose of your own medicine? After about twenty seconds it moved off as if nothing had happened.

Five or six of us, having taken up positions behind the grille, were doing our best to return the heavy fire, but the enemy was well hidden. We just fired at any window, hoping to hit somebody.

Then we were spotted by observers in the old castle, and immediately there was an intensive mortar attack. Three bombs fell to our left, fragments whistled past our ears, and we flattened ourselves to the ground in an attempt to take deeper cover in the bushes. Another three bombs came over, much closer, then three more less than fifteen yards away. This time we knew they were after us, so I ordered everybody back to the shelter of the Casino.

This reception had made us sweat a bit. The next three bombs hit the roof of the building just west of the shed: the enemy had shortened their range a little too much. The mortar men were evidently lacking in experience, or they would simply have fired three rapid rounds and the bombs would have hit us.

After a minute or two the mortar fire stopped, and we moved cautiously back to our positions in the bushes. I regretted bitterly not having one of my mortars: the Germans in the old castle and on the cliff would not have had such an easy time of it. Nothing was working out as planned.

A soldier warned me that his companion had been killed just near us, and that there was probably a sniper in the steeple of the church of St Rémy which overlooked the beach about 300 yards away. There was a slight movement behind the stone columns of the cupola. I sent a soldier for an anti-tank rifle that someone had abandoned in the bushes a little further along. He brought it back with some magazines he had found with it, but the bolt was missing. We had a look around but could not find it. No doubt the soldier who threw the rifle away took the bolt out deliberately so that the enemy could not use it.

One of the soldiers had a machine-gun, and I borrowed it. I had a good firing position close to the little wall, and taking careful aim, I fired two long bursts at the steeple. By instinct I moved about two feet to the right and in no time a bullet hit just where I had been lying. I emptied the magazine, put on a fresh one, and emptied that too. There was no answer to my fire: either the sniper had been hit, or he had decided that the place was unhealthy.

I took a few minutes' rest, which I badly needed. So far I had been doing my soldiers' work instead of my own, fighting instead of commanding; but there had been no alternative. Of my forty-five men, there were four with me. That was all; the others were scattered all over the place. A good many had stayed on the beach, wounded, dead, or playing dead. It was impossible, in the pandemonium, to do anything about re-organizing my platoon.

So far, too, I had been involved with the preceding wave rather than with my own battalion. I should report to the CO, but where was HQ? The CO's R-craft had landed over to the right, so he should be west of the Casino and still on the beach, because nobody could get off it with some 300 yards of open esplanade to cross. There were some khaki figures lying there, but I could not make out who they were. I could only hope that the CO had been lucky.

Further along on our left I recognized three privates from my platoon who had stayed together and appeared to be un-wounded: Ulric, who was responsible for maps and com-munications, Maréchal, my range-taker, and Simard, a number three mortar man. They were trying to get into the city on their own. As this took a lot of courage, I was proud of them: they were really fighting. I saw them leave the cover of the top of the beach together and make a mad dash ascross the esplanade.

They were soon separated by their speed. Ulric, who was the tallest, was first; then came Maréchal, of medium height, while Simard, who was no more than five feet, was last.

A machine-gun opened up on them. Ulric had reached the wall and hugged it, out of reach. Maréchal fell, badly wounded. The machine-gun had ripped his belly wide open and he was holding his guts in with both hands. Simard had spun round and gone back to the cover of the edge of the esplanade.

The firing had stopped. Maréchal was writhing in full view, in mortal pain and yelling for help. Simard could not leave his companion there, so he jumped up and ran out to him. Even though he was short, he was strong, and in a quick fireman's lift he picked his friend up and dashed back to cover with him through a renewed hail of bullets.

This act of heroism, however, was useless. Maréchal's guts were spilling out and dragging on the ground. There was no hope for him. Simard knew this and was powerless to do anything more about it. Ulric rushed back, unwounded; he arrived in time to see his friend die.

I returned to the big hall of the Casino. Vermette was kneeling in the centre of the bay window, which had been cleared of its glass several hours earlier. He had lost his steel helmet, and his left ear had been cut horizontally right across the centre. The two pieces were cleanly separated and the wound had marked the skin on each side. He was bleeding badly, but did not seem to notice it. He was too busy! He was in full view of the enemy, firing his machine-gun at some targets on the cliff. There was a pile of empty magazines around him.

His gun was misfiring. He cleared it twice and resumed shooting, but not for long. It jammed again and this time it would not start after being cleared.

'What's wrong?' I asked.

His tone of voice when he answered was not that of the old quiet Lance Corporal Vermette, always . calm, even timid, whom Sergeant Brunet baited endlessly. Something had changed 'Pop' Vermette. His eyes were starting out of his head, he was dribbling, he had no time even to swallow his saliva. He was foaming with rage, so mad altogether that he hardly knew what he was doing.

'I'd like to meet the bastard who invented this bastard of a bren-gun. I'd kill the bastard. . . .' The litany went on.

'Your gun is dirty, the carbon is clogging up the regulator, you'll have to stop and clean it.'

'The f——g regulator is fully open.'

'It's clogged. Break it down and put the wire brush through it.'

'I haven't got time. I've Germans to kill.'

'Take time. I'll cover you with a rifle.'

All I got for an answer was a spluttering of swear-words, but he did start to clean his gun, and I fired rapidly into the bushes in front of the old castle to keep the German heads down. We were getting a few bursts in answer, some bullets whistling right through the window, others hitting the edges all the way round. The firing was sporadic, which meant that they were not feeling very safe.

I had taken up a position at the left-hand corner of the window, while Vermette, cleaning his gun, was sitting right in the middle. I had to insist he moved aside; I did not want him killed needlessly.

The cleaning was quickly done and the gun remounted. Vermette had half a smile on his face as he fired a trial burst; the gun was working well. As he resumed his harassment of the enemy, I spotted a movement in the bushes and directed his fire there. He was running short of ammo, so I fetched him some from the back of the Casino.

It was now 0930 hours. The enemy fire had died down a little while ours seemed to be increasing. This must have been because we were getting used to being fired on; the officers and NCOs were taking the men in hand and organizing the firing. Nobody, however, had time to look after the wounded; they lay where they fell, and many died for lack of care.

One of the small boats that had landed under the cliff on our right was completely ripped open by machine-gun fire. It had great holes in its sides, and looking down from this upper window we could see the bodies in it. They must have fought desperately, and had all been killed. Some of the survivors of 'A' Coy were ashore under the cliff, and as I could see the Germans dropping grenades on them from above, I told the riflemen who were firing from the second floor to try and get them.

All our troops seemed to have landed, but we were fighting alongside complete strangers, men not only from other battalions but from other sections altogether. There were tank men, pioneers, engineers, signallers, despatch riders. It was quite a mixed-up affair, and although we tried to reorganize ourselves, the battle would have had to stop for us to be able to do this properly.

I was getting very tired. I still had my big pack full of ammo on my back. I wanted to use my binoculars, and when I dragged my handkerchief out to clean them, I saw it was soaked with sweat. By rights I should have been dead hours ago; I must be bullet-proof. The thought gave me renewed strength. Dozens of my friends and companions had been less lucky. I was seething with the lust for vengeance.

4

A soldier told me that two men who tried to cross a passage that led into the street, had got themselves shot. I returned to the shed where the Lieutenant was still trying to get in touch with his superior officers. As he could not get through, I suggested he try mine, but there was no luck there either.

I made my way down to the beach again. This time it seemed to be quite easy. I knew just where to get the most protection. I ran from the north wall of the Casino to the blockhouse; and after waiting a minute to fool the enemy, I dashed down to the front of the burning TLC. There, screened by the ship, I signalled and yelled for everyone to join me. Some wounded who were still able to fight were resting behind the TLC and I persuaded them to come up and give covering fire from the Casino windows.

The return trip was a complete success; we did not give the enemy any advance warning, and we all managed to make it across the dangerous open space. I looked for some 2-inch mortar bombs on the beach, so as to lay a smoke screen and be able to carry on into the city, but there was none to be found.

I posted every available man at the windows of the Casino, and the sergeant would make sure we got maximum covering fire over the wall. Seven of us were going to have a crack at getting into the city; we got set just like long-distance runners and then we were off. The Germans did not even open fire on us. However, only six men got across the esplanade: the seventh had stumbled and fallen, and was scrambling on all fours to get back to the cover of the passage. The enemy guns opened up, but they were much too late. We were safely across, and out of reach if we stayed close to the wall. It was about eight feet high, and we were going to have to help each other over.

Supporting fire came over our heads, but we lobbed a couple of grenades all the same just in case there were any Germans on the other side. As we climbed over, we could see a small anti-tank gun at the next corner. This came as a surprise; it had not been there before, or we should have seen it from the Casino. Luckily for us, at least two of our brens were firing at it and the crew were ducked behind the apron. We ran towards the gun, three on each side of the street for mutual protection.

When we were thirty yards away, and getting ready to throw grenades, one of the crew risked a look round the edge of the apron and saw us almost on top of them. He let out a loud yell, at which they all abandoned the gun and fled into a street on the right.

As the gun had a shell in the chamber, we fired it at the old castle; the shot went too low, but it might have scared the enemy. We had no explosives to destroy the gun, so we tried reversing a shell in the muzzle and firing a grenade in the chamber, but the only effect was to send the shell flying ten feet away. We had no more time to waste on this caper.

Our aim being to establish our platoon HQ in the steeple of St Rémy Church, we headed in that direction.

Three shots were fired at us in quick succession, and one of us fell, wounded in the leg; but he was quickly on his feet again limping towards the corner of the street. At the sound of the shots, we had jumped into doorways and flattened ourselves along the walls; this gave us some sort of cover while still allowing a relatively good firing position. We could not tell where the shots had come from, and that is always rather unnerving. As soon as we came out in the open they would open fire again.

The wounded man had made his way across the street and jumped over a low iron fence into the churchyard. Watching closely, he fired into a window on the east side of the road. Thinking he was just nervous, we resumed our advance, but as we came under the window a stick grenade landed at our feet. We all jumped for cover; two men fell and did not get up.

Corporal Lebel and I were both on the left-hand side of the street, so I dashed across to support the sole survivor on the other side. As he went forward he was knocked down by a burst of sub-machine-gun fire. The fact was there were Germans in practically every house, and to be of any use we should have to clear them all out one after another.

We certainly did not have the men to do this, and in any case it would not be long before we were all killed, to no avail. Lebel and I therefore backed down the street towards the corner and the church. We were about to jump the fence when I realized how stupid it was to try and get into the church: the Germans were guarding the approaches and would probably have a reception committee inside as well.

We returned to the Casino by the same route, helping our casualty, and we were lucky not to get fired at. Our only danger was from our own machine-guns, which gave us quite a scare as they opened up, firing to our front and into all the windows they could reach, and for a time we were caught in the middle of their ricochets.

By the time we had carried our man into the Casino, he was just about passing out, and we handed him over to his sergeant in the RHLI. He had a bullet through his thigh, although amazingly the bone was not broken.

One of our corporals from No. 4 platoon told me that Sergeant Michaud had had trouble with one of my men, Casimir Dubord. This surprised me rather, as Dubord was a good soldier; and, in fact as I discovered, the truth was rather different from the report. Far from lagging back, Dubord had gone fighting mad. He was with a group from No. 4 platoon, under Sergeant Michaud, when they met some Germans. In a fierce close-quarter fight they came out the winners; when it was over

Michaud found Dubord kneeling on one of the Germans, locking his arms behind his back and trying to hack off his head with his bayonet. The sergeant intervened.

'Stop that, Dubord, and come along.' Dubord merely swore at him and continued with his crude butchery. Michaud realized that Dubord had gone crazy with rage, and slapped him across the face.

'Now, get a move on.' For a second, Dubord was dumb-founded; then he stuck his bayonet in the German's back and joined the others.

It seemed that the quiet, timid older fellows were not sitting back waiting for somebody else to do a job. They were at the front, while many of the loud-mouthed braggarts had been shown up for what they were. It was easy to get the men to lie down—if they waited for the signal, that is; more difficult to persuade them to get up and advance. They froze to the ground even when common sense should have told them to get under cover. But in a fight like this, common sense did not always apply. Discipline is the only thing that makes soldiers move when they are scared.

Back at the shed, the officer had still not received any orders. At that moment, our aircraft swooped down and laid a smoke screen over the beach, but it quickly drifted away seaward. It was 1100 hours: re-embarkation time. The boats should be at the beach within five minutes.

The officer, ordering all weapons lying about to be heaped in a pile, instructed a soldier from the Engineers to blow the lot up. We assembled all the men, including those on the second floor of the Casino, who could not see that the boats had come. As many of the wounded as possible were being helped, although some who were too far gone would have to be left behind as we had no time to evacuate them; in any case, they would have a better chance of getting quick first aid if they stayed there.

The officer and I were staying behind to protect the evacuation, each with a bren-gun and plenty of full magazines. To start with, I fired a full pack into all the windows that looked out on the beach. The enemy had at all costs to be kept down.

As soon as the ALCs came in, the men ran down to the

1 The area around the casino and the port in Dieppe where the Canadian attack went in

2 The approach to Dieppe: Allied landing craft under fire

3   The burning Tank Landing Craft into which the author ran several times to help the wounded and where he finally surrendered

4   The aftermath of the assault of the beach

5   The aftermath of the assault on the edge of the town

6   Allied troops being marshalled following their surrender

7 The author on his return from North Africa when he received the Military Medal for his part in the Dieppe Raid

water's edge, and the moment the ramps were lowered they rushed the boats, some of which were soon so overloaded they could not get off the beach; but trying to make any of the men disembark was a waste of time. The one thing they wanted was to escape from the hellish fire, which had then risen to a crescendo. The Germans, determined to prevent the evacuation, were shooting with every weapon they had, causing many casualties.

The officer and I made our way down to the beach, ready to fire at any German who appeared. A corporal of No. 4 platoon of my battalion was lying badly wounded in both thighs and unable to move. He called out to me:

'PSM, for God's sake don't leave me here! Take me back to England!'

'O.K., let's go.'

He was a big man, much too heavy for me to carry, but it was bad enough having to leave the wounded who were unconscious. Having ordered some German prisoners to give me a hand with him, we carried him down to the water's edge. He suffered terribly from the handling, which was far from gentle. Fortunately there was half a rubber-foam raft floating nearby, and we were able to lay him on it and push him towards the nearest boat, which was about forty yards away. The ramp was lowered and the prisoners helped lift the wounded man on board. I did not know what would happen to the prisoners, and I did not care. It was high time to get on board myself, as the vessel was about to push off.

There was a rope hanging over the side, which I grabbed, for I had forgotten about the load on my back, and the pack had filled with water. Try as I might, I just could not pull myself up, and the boat was gathering speed. I yelled for help from the men on board, but with all the noise, they could not hear me.

Before the boat got into deep water, I let go of the rope.

CHAPTER THREE

Capture

1

I SANK like a rock, for my Mae West was only half inflated. I was in about nine feet of water and there was no question of swimming. I tried to get rid of my equipment, but I had fastened it too well. The only thing that would come off was my steel helmet, and as it probably contained some air it was not weighing me down.

I jumped towards the surface and managed to snatch a quick breath of air, but sank again at once. I was getting less and less buoyant. I was choking! The salt water and the sweat on my face were stinging my eyes.

After several hours of heavy fighting in which I had risked death any number of times, it seemed I was going to drown accidentally. I said to myself,

'Well, Lucien old bean, this is where you finish your life, in the dirty waters of Dieppe.'

Then, with ears humming, I lost consciousness.

I came to with my head out of the water. Before I passed out, I had started to push towards the beach with my feet and arms. The wash of the boats on each side of me must have helped to propel me ashore. Our training had certainly helped; I probably kept on making the effort, without knowing it.

I had swallowed a lot of water, and now I was sick. As I advanced very slowly, the fresh air began to do me good, but I was still very groggy.

When the water was about up to my knees, I woke up to the

fact that a machine-gun was firing at me; bullets were hitting the water all around me. I could have dropped below the surface and lain there with only my face showing, but I was past caring.

So I staggered on through the rain of bullets, and suddenly found myself in the shelter of the burning TLC. My body crumpled; I was just a heap of wet clothes on the beach. After a minute or so, I took my equipment off; I did not think I should need it any more. In the water I had tried to reach into my right-hand trouser pocket for a sharp penknife I carried, but the pressure was too much for me to slide my hand in. Even now, it was difficult to get the knife out; my wet clothes hindered my movements.

Gradually my head cleared, and when I began to consider the situation I realized that things were not very bright. There were a number of men lying in the lee of the TLC, most of them seriously wounded. I stood up, and my fighting spirit began to surge back. Though very tired, I had to organize the defence of the ship. So far, the exploding ammunition inside it had prevented anybody from going aboard; but it would make a good shelter for the wounded.

For the moment, the enemy were leaving us alone, and were concentrating their fire on the ships that had come in to re-embark the troops. From the safety of the TLC I could watch the sea, and I pitied the fellows out there. They were taking an awful pasting, not only from the guns and mortars but also now from the Luftwaffe. Earlier on, enemy aircraft seemed to have been kept away by our planes, but now they were there in force, without serious opposition. The sea was being churned up by bombs and shells. There were several direct hits, and many of the boats were swamped by near misses.

Although all the ships had left the beach and we had therefore no hope of being taken off, I could not help willing them away out of that hellish fire. If they could once get clear of the coast they would come under the protection of the Navy's ack-ack guns, and, later on, of the RAF.

Amongst the survivors on the beach were Lieutenant Bissonette and Corporal Desaulniers of our battalion. The corporal had a head wound; his face was so bloody I didn't recognize him and he had to tell me his name, but his morale was unaffected. There were three or four other men from our battalion, all seriously wounded, and ten or twelve others from different units.

There was also a doctor. He would not be of any help militarily, but we could certainly use him. He had no more dressings or other medical supplies, but before embarking the previous night we had each been given a personal first-aid kit containing morphine. We were supposed to keep it for our own use, but there was little likelihood of my being wounded, having lived through all this, and so I handed it over. It would not go far among so many, but some at least would get immediate relief.

As I was very thirsty after swallowing all that sea water, I pulled out my water bottle, which was still full. Suddenly I was aware of all the wounded men looking at me. One finally said:

'When you've finished, PSM, will you let me have a drink?'

I felt very ashamed of having drunk good water, when there were wounded men who had been thirsty for hours. There was hope yet, however: inside the TLC I had noticed a lot of soldiers' equipment lying about. The doctor said I could not go in there; I should just be another casualty, but it had to be tried.

There was a curtain of fire from the exploding ammo but I got through it at a run. The air was so hot inside that I had to hold my breath, and my hair caught fire as I had no steel helmet. Luckily my hair was very short, and a slap on the head put the fire out. Grabbing two water bottles I ran for it. Rifle bullets spattered the hull as the fire reached them, like a continuous barrage of fire-crackers, with, every now and again, the louder explosion of a shell.

I escaped without serious injury, but gasping for air. The wounded were glad of the water even though it was warm; they had been lying in the hot sun most of the morning.

As the Germans had little opposition by now, I knew they would try to come down on to the beach. To prevent them, I posted two machine-guns, one at each end of the ship. The gunners were an unwounded sergeant and a private who was only slightly hurt. I gave them orders not to fire until the enemy started coming down.

The wounded were feverish and needed blankets. The fire inside the TLC had abated somewhat, and I managed to fetch blankets and half-a-dozen water bottles. I had a good drink myself this time.

At 1300 hours the area was beginning to quieten down, and there was little firing. It was a long time since the boats had come and gone, filled to overflowing, and they were not coming back! Some of the boats had been torn apart on the beach; others had foundered and the incoming tide was washing over them. Bodies were lying all over the beach; some were floating in the water, others, weighted down, were being submerged like the boats. What a sight!

Suddenly a destroyer raced into view and came speeding towards the beach, firing as it came. It stopped 250 yards offshore, defying the enemy with its guns. An officer came down from the bridge and signalled to the soldiers on the beach to swim out to the ship. I recognized him; he was the GOC 2nd Canadian Division, General Roberts. So he had not abandoned us after all!

Some of the soldiers undressed and swam to the ship, and we could see the sailors pulling them up with ropes. I knew I should never make it. I was not a good swimmer at the best of times, and I was in no condition to try it now.

After waiting about ten minutes, the destroyer turned seaward and slowly disappeared.

2

Now there was not a ship to be seen and we were quite alone. The sea was coming in and would soon reach us. The enemy were still firing in a leisurely way at any group showing activity on the beach. We were being shot at too, but they could not reach us as we were protected by the hull of the TLC which was tilted seaward.

Eventually the incoming tide would drive us out. We could not go into the ship, for she was still on fire and ammo was still exploding. We should have to go back to the Casino, and that was not possible: there were not enough men to carry the wounded, and anyway the Germans were probably in there by now.

The wounded were beginning to get their feet wet from the waves. The MO advised me that we should have to surrender soon, or the men would drown. Although he was a captain, he gave me no orders—indeed he had no right to. I was the one who had organized the defence, and it was up to me to decide whether we were to cease fighting.

This was a terrible decision to have to make. We should have fought to the last man and the last breath. We had come so far to fight, and all our thoughts had been turned to this objective for three years. Now somebody was suggesting surrender—and I did not shoot him down!

We had sufficient weapons and ammo to keep the enemy at bay, and so far we had been successful. True, they had not made any particular efforts in our direction. Twice some soldiers had appeared at the Casino, but a few shots from the machine-gun in single rounds had been enough to send them packing. The noise from the exploding ammo probably led them to believe that there were quite a few of us, and that we were firing continuously.

However, now that the Germans had had time to analyse the situation, there was certain to be a concerted attack on us, and they would soon find out that we could not defend the other side of the ship.

We could hold out for a little longer, but what would be the point? It would not be for glory, because nobody would ever know anything about this last stand. Would it be for a soldier's honour? It would not be an honour to let these wounded men drown. I was responsible for their lives; was I to sacrifice them for the sake of my personal pride?

The MO had left me time to think this out, but as if he knew the decision in advance, he was preparing a white cloth on the end of a stick.

'Well, Sergeant-Major? It'll soon be too late.'

At last, and almost against my will, I answered,

'Yes, sir, we are surrendering.'

The terrible words had been pronounced. Never would I have believed I should say them! Never did I suspect I should surrender to the enemy. Was it duty or fear that forced me to this step? Certainly I was afraid. I was afraid of what would happen to me in the hands of the enemy, but not for my skin. I was afraid of having to live with my conscience after surrendering in my first engagement.

Well, if it was my duty, I would do it. It would have been too easy to let the officer show the white flag and then pretend that he, not I, had surrendered. I would not allow this, so I picked up a rifle with a bayonet on it and tied my handkerchief to the end. It was an old khaki handkerchief that had turned yellow with age, so I did not even capitulate under a white flag, but under a yellow rag, the colour of cowardice!

The MO went to the forepart of the vessel, but passing him, I went inside and climbed on to the upper deck, where I should be in full view of the enemy. I waved my flag—and was promptly greeted with rifle fire! That was almost enough to cause me to bring down the rifle and answer them in kind; but I remembered the wounded, and hiding myself, continued to wave the flag. Every minute counted.

Some Germans finally showed themselves at the top of the beach, to the left of the Casino, and the MO, wearing a Red Cross armband and waving his white flag, went towards them.

One of the Germans was yelling at me, but I could not understand him. Then he gestured to me to throw down the rifle and raise my hands. Since I had asked to surrender, I could not make the least aggressive movement. I took the handkerchief from the bayonet and threw the rifle down on to the shingle. The bayonet dug itself in and the rifle stuck, butt end up; the way we mark the spot where a soldier lies wounded or dead. It seemed to symbolize the fact that my military life was over.

I climbed down from the hull and went to the lee side where the wounded were lying, and ordered those who could move to help one another up to the top of the beach. The German soldier was yelling at the other end of the ship, not daring to come into our view. Only when he saw the first wounded was he reassured.

47

Some we just pulled up to the end of the ship so that they would be out of the water. On our first trip up to the Casino, the enemy were very nervous, and kept prodding us with their rifles. After laying down our wounded, we picked up some stretchers and started to go back for the worst cases, but the Germans wanted us to raise our hands and go on up. The men, realizing they were liable to be shot if they did not obey, hesitated, but I had to keep control if the collection of our wounded was to be completed and not left to the Germans; at any moment an extra big wave might drown them. I told the men:

'We have surrendered to save our wounded, not to save our own lives. About turn and back to the ship!'

At this they picked up two stretchers and headed back to the beach. Seeing me giving orders, one of the Germans jabbed his bayonet against my stomach. I felt like showing him how fast I could make his rifle fly, but where would that have got me? I knew that German soldiers feared their sergeant-majors, and I decided to put on a show of authority. I stood up to my full height, and told him, in a voice that brooked no argument:

'*Ich bin ein Kanadische Hauptfeldwebel.*' (I am a Canadian sergeant-major.)

The look I gave him as I pointed to the crown on my sleeve made him back away and bring down his rifle. For a second I thought that he was going to salute me! I pushed my advantage:

'*Wir haben vielen Verwundeten, wir kommen mit zurück, bringen Sie ihr Feldwebel.*' (We have many wounded, we are bringing them back, get your sergeant.)

Then, turning my back on him, I started down towards the TLC. After several more trips, the last of our wounded were brought safely to the top of the beach. I wanted to go further afield to pick up other casualties, but the soldier this time was very firm and I realized that if I persisted he would most certainly shoot me.

Resignedly, I raised my hands above my head and turned towards the town.

We joined the lugubrious gathering of prisoners in the park in front of the Dieppe hospital. Several of them were wounded but still able to walk. On their field dressings the blood was showing, the wounds sticking to the cloth. These dressings, bright with blood, made a light note against the drabness of the uniforms. The seriously wounded had already been taken into this civilian hospital, where nuns and doctors, French and German, were treating them.

All of us were exhausted and many unshaven, our faces stained with dust, blood and sweat, and betraying the strain of battle as well as the bitterness of capture. Many, like myself, had been in the sea, and our uniforms were torn, dirty and sodden. Some were down to their underwear.

We looked like a beaten army, and I hated to be seen in that state by the French population.

Next, our captors searched us. I managed to keep my jack-knife; its sharp little blade might come in handy later on. We were then assembled into a marching column. Suddenly one of our soldiers stepped out of the ranks holding a grenade in his hand. The Germans ran in every direction. He dropped the grenade on the ground, simply to get rid of it, and we could all see that the pin had not been pulled. A gust of laughter shook the ranks; the Germans did not seem at all pleased.

We set off marching in a south-easterly direction out of the town of Dieppe. We were all desperately thirsty, for the day was hot, and we had had no food and little to drink—apart from salt water!—since morning. But the Germans were clearly in a great hurry to get us out of Dieppe. It must be remembered that they had not expected our visit and had therefore made no provision for feeding us.

Throughout the march, they kept the French population away, and all we could do was help our wounded as best we could, and encourage them to carry on.

When we arrived at the small village of Saint-Martin-l'Eglise, the German *Feldgendarmerie* who were guarding us at last allowed the inhabitants to give us some water. It was then 1700 hours. After a halt at the side of the road, we were taken to a sports field, where two squads of *Jägertruppen* took over as escorts.

They were sixteen and seventeen years old, and at first we did not take them for soldiers at all. Their chins had certainly not seen a razor yet; they looked more like boys playing at being soldiers. In fact, we thought they were cadets brought to sneer at us; but no, they were soldiers of the great Reich. Their NCOs, however, looked and acted like real soldiers.

Since our capture, I had been acting as interpreter, as none of our guards spoke either French or English. This was not for their convenience, but for mine; it was part of a plan of escape I had been formulating. I calculated that if I made myself the only link between ourselves and the Germans, I should be allowed more liberty; and so it worked out. I was kept out of the ranks, and marched alongside the man in command. However, it worked both ways, because every time something came up, they turned to me. Thus I was under constant watch, and if I disappeared, they would know about it at once.

Realizing this, when we formed up again to resume our march, I joined my comrades in the ranks, and hoped that the old guard had not informed their successors of my ability to speak a little German. Apparently they had not, for nobody came searching for me.

One group consisted of several hundred prisoners, some of whom, having taken off their boots to swim to the ships, were barefoot. Luckily some of us still had our Mae Wests on, and we cut them up to make sandals. My knife came in handy for this, but we had to take care that the Germans did not spot it. Others had only their underwear on, and some of us took off our shirts to dress them. The French population succeeded in passing on some old trousers to us.

We got the feeling that the French had a lot of sympathy for us and were doing their best to help us. How they must have hated the Germans! Any chance of liberation had been frustrated by our capture; we hoped with them that the next time it would be different. We knew that the tide of war was changing, and I longed to be able to tell them not to despair. Their friendly faces were a great comfort to us in our plight.

As evening came our misery increased. We had been at full stretch since early morning, and had good reason to be tired. Wearily we approached another village, called Envermeu, but we marched on through it and out the other side. We wondered when we were going to stop. A few miles further on we came to a factory under construction, and at last we were halted. This, it seemed, was the hotel the *Wehrmacht* had reserved for us.

Soon afterwards we were given food: a loaf of black bread each. We had heard about the German army's rye-bread, but we had never thought it could be as bad as this. The outside of the loaf was a dirty rough brown, and if it had not been for its rounded top edges, it could well have been taken for a brick. The inside was a squodgy, very dark dough, and it tasted revolting. It seemed hard to believe they liked it and ate it habitually, but we couldn't afford to be fussy. I didn't eat much of mine, not because of the taste, but because I was already making provision for my future escape. At least, I thought, this clay-like substance should keep well!

Our group had swollen to about 800, and I was horrified at the number of us who had been taken prisoner, some of them old comrades. I knew that things had gone badly in my sector, but had never dreamed that the whole operation had gone wrong on such a large scale.

Late in the evening a very dark brew was brought to us. Although it was called *kaffee* by the Germans, and was hot, it smelt and tasted of rubber. If this was what they were reduced to for coffee, they must be in a poor way.

After this, we were told to go into the factory for the night. Some of our boys wanted more water and refused to move. The Germans started to push them back towards the door; there was rebellion in the air and I could see a fight brewing. The situation was tense; but after a while the NCOs succeeded in cooling the men down, and persuaded them to go into the unfinished factory. A little later a doctor arrived and demanded to see the wounded. He looked at about ten of them, but did not undo a single bandage, try to help any of them or even send any to the hospital, and we realized he was just curious. Soon the senior officer put a stop to it by telling the wounded not to come out. The 'doctor' departed, and our casualties resigned themselves to spending the night where they were.

It was going to be no luxury hotel. There were no beds, and the floor was unfinished; it consisted of large rocks crushed to form a foundation for concrete, that was all. The most sheltered corner was reserved for the wounded, and some boards were found and laid down as a platform to protect them from the hard edges of the rocks. There was no glass in the windows; and as we expected the night to be cool, we lent them bits of clothing to cover them up. Most of them were feverish, and their dressings badly needed to be changed.

I picked a spot and levelled it a bit, and selected a large comfortable-looking stone for a pillow. I covered myself with my blouse, and my last thought as I stretched out on my rocky bed was that I should not get much sleep. I woke up once during the night, simply to turn over on to the other side.

4

In the morning the sun was shining; I woke up feeling refreshed, if a bit 'rocky'. We were allowed to go out in the yard. I had already decided that, for me, the war was not going to finish in a prisoner-of-war camp. Today I intended to start seriously investigating the possibilities of escape.

The factory was surrounded by open fields, but there was a seven foot wire fence round the yard, with a guard every twenty feet. Some French people tried to come close enough to talk to us, under the pretext of gathering grass for their rabbits, but the guards chased them away.

Several ideas came to me as I inspected the premises. A concrete mixer, a pile of rocks, and a small window leading into a sort of cellar, all at first seemed to have potential, but there were snags. I should have to wait for a better chance.

During the day we had quite a lot of visitors: German generals and staff officers. Some of them spoke French, and we had to answer a lot of questions. We felt like animals in a zoo.

I wanted to employ my time doing something useful, and it

occurred to me that perhaps a bit of propaganda would not be wasted. So I wandered over to one of the guards and started a conversation through the fence. After a while I asked him— as one soldier to another—whether he liked the army. He glanced round to see if his comrades were within earshot; then he said no, he didn't. I told him we were all volunteers from Canada, and that in the British and Canadian armies we ate only white bread, with meat twice a day. He admitted they didn't often see meat, and got only twenty cigarettes a week.

'Too bad,' I murmured, 'I only wish I'd brought the 1500 cigarettes I left behind in my pack in England.'

But I could see he didn't believe me.

In the afternoon an Intelligence officer came to interrogate some of the prisoners. He chose six who seemed to be the youngest and most co-operative, among them 'Baby Face' Rousseau of my platoon. He had a soft, round, rather angelic face —and was one of the toughest sergeants we had. I hoped the others would prove as tough as he.

When he came out, Rousseau said the officer had told him that the Germans had been expecting the raid for the past month, and had photographs taken during our training on the Isle of Wight. Perhaps. I warned the others to keep their mouths shut.

5

Around 1600 hours we were formed up into column of route and marched out of the camp. As before I was on the look-out for a chance to get away, but there was not a hope! Although Corporal Vermette, who was also a prisoner, and I took the right-hand file, nearest the side of the road, the guards' vigilance was never relaxed long enough for us to make a dash for it.

We were led to the railroad station where a freight train was waiting in a siding. The cars were cattle-trucks; this was the first time we had been treated like cattle. Vermette and I managed to be in the same car, with eighteen others. The doors were locked on the outside. One car out of three was left empty for the guards, who were equipped with rifles, machine-guns and sub-machine-guns. We were well guarded; yet I was certain there was a loophole in their security system, if only I could find it.

The train started, and some time later we went rolling through Dieppe. Only yesterday we had been there as free men. In Rouen, as in Dieppe, the word had got around that we were coming, and the French population was lining the tracks to cheer us. Some of the women were crying. I suppose we represented defeat after an unsuccessful invasion attempt.

In the meantime I set to work. With the help of several of the men I succeeded in lifting a plank from the floor. This gave us a way out, but it was just in front of the rear wheels of the car. Since the axle turned with the wheels, we could not use it for support, and there was not enough height between the track and the axle to allow us to fall clear of it. We put the plank back; we should have to find another exit.

One of the prisoners in our car seemed to be making signs out of the window to the guards in the car ahead. Although he was wearing British battledress, no-one knew him. So Corporal Vermette, who spoke good English, engaged him in conversation. He said that he belonged to No. 6 Commando, that he had landed at 0400 hours at Dieppe, and that he came from Glasgow. Since he did not have the faintest trace of a Scots accent and his English was very bad, and anyway there were no commandos from 6 Coy on the raid, we realized he was a spy.

Our first idea was to throw him out through the hole in the floor; but this might have attracted the attention of the guards, and they might have guessed what we were up to. The sergeant-major said that he and his men would keep an eye on him, and if he gave any trouble they would quietly throttle him.

Before we left England we had been given an escape course by special Intelligence officers. One thing they told us was that there were organizations on the Continent helping shot-down airmen of the Allied forces to return to England. Obviously they could not give us the addresses of these people, but, should we ever need them, they said we should look around and not despair.

Vermette was very keen to escape with me, and now Cloutier,

also from my platoon, asked if he could join us. I agreed; three are not too many in an escape. We set to work to remove a plank that barred one of the windows on the right-hand side of the truck. After a struggle it came away. This gave us a means of escape when the time came; but for the moment we put it back and held it there and awaited our chance.

After we had travelled through Rouen, the moon, which had been shining brightly, went behind a cloud. At the same time the track curved to the left, so that our window was hidden from the guards in the front and rear, even if they stretched their necks. This was it! We were off!

In a second I was out through the opening, followed by Vermette and Cloutier. Hand over fist we got between the cars on to the buffers; but the train was travelling too fast for us to jump in safety. At that moment we passed through a small station where there were German soldiers on the platforms. We pressed ourselves against the end of the truck in an effort to become invisible. Everybody seemed to be staring at us as we clung there motionless, but the train carried on and there was no alert. Another station; the same thing again, and again we were not spotted. A few miles later the train started to climb, and slowed down to about twenty-five miles an hour. The time had come.

I grasped the lower part of the left-hand window and hung there, feeling for the ballast. My toes touched it and I felt the speed of the train. Three feet away, parallel to the track, was a signal wire. Landing on my feet, I did a neat somersault over the wire and twisted in mid-air so that I came down on the sloping edge of the ballast, on my stomach and facing the train. The whole thing had taken probably three seconds.

I stayed down so that the guards would not see me, and to give Vermette and Cloutier a chance to get away too; just then somebody started shooting at me. Bullets were whistling all around me. I was not sure where the firing was coming from, but it might have been from beside the track. Anyway, it was time to get away—and fast.

In three leaps I was down the embankment, and clearing the five foot fence at the bottom with one hand lightly on a post. I had never been so agile; being short and stocky I am not a born sprinter or jumper, but the way I made that somersault and vaulted that fence, one would think I had had wings instead of feet.

Luckily there was a forest close to the track and I was instantly out of sight among the trees. I ran for about twenty-five yards, and hurling myself into a particularly thick bush lay still. I wanted any pursuer to lose track of me if he was listening to the sound of my running. I held my breath and listened intently.

CHAPTER FOUR

Friends in Need

1

THERE was no sound except the train rumbling in the distance, and the shots getting further and further away, but to be on the safe side I made a detour to get back to the railway line. It had been arranged that I should jump first and then walk towards the others who would come back towards me. As I climbed the embankment, I heard somebody coming along the tracks and I dodged behind a bush. It was probably my two companions; still, I was taking no chances.

Just as well: it wasn't Vermette and Cloutier at all, but two French railroad guards. At the same time I heard Cloutier yelling:

'Sergeant-Major Dumais!'

The call came a second time, and it was not very far away. I was amazed that the guards didn't hear it, but then they weren't listening and were making a lot of noise as they marched. As soon as they had passed, I climbed up to the ballast and shouted back.

No answer. I ran along beside the track, calling as I went. No answer. Another seventy yards and I stopped. They couldn't be any further than this. I called out again, loudly, in my best sergeant-major's voice. Still no answer.

What was happening? Perhaps for some reason they couldn't answer me, so I went to and fro whistling *Un Canadien Errant*, an old French Canadian song, the first bar of which is our Regimental bugle call. No Frenchman or German would recognize it. I stopped, waited and listened. Silence.

They must have dodged into the forest immediately after calling out the second time, but where? I knew they hadn't passed me, so they might have started running in the same direction as the train. I jog-trotted along beside the tracks for ten minutes and called out again. There was no answering shout. I had lost my companions.

2

I was alone on French soil, still in my Canadian uniform, surrounded by the enemy and without resources. I took stock of the situation. I was free, and that was something. The Germans had not kept me long. Now I had to get back to England.

I had been following the train in a southerly direction, and I thought I might just as well keep going. The local German troops would have been alerted, and they would be sure to search for us in the area where we had escaped. Once I was outside that zone, I should be safer. I also had to get out of the forest. I should only get lost in it, and reduce my chances of finding help.

My big, hobnailed boots were making a lot of noise on the sleepers, so I took them off, tied the laces together and hung them round my neck, leaving my hands free. My heavy woollen socks were much too big originally but had now shrunk down to size; they were more like heavy felt, and protected my feet splendidly. In my blouse I had three-quarters of a loaf of German bread; too bad I hadn't saved my escape kit instead of distributing it among my men. It would have come in handy now.

Marching fast, keeping on the sleepers, in the dark of the now moonless night, I was a mere passing shadow. Yet, even at that late hour, there were still people travelling, like me, on the tracks. I quickly came to recognize the slow, heavy footsteps of the railroad guards, talking between themselves, and I slipped down the embankment to let them go by. But there were also other, less definite, footsteps, whose owners I preferred not to meet. Once they were past I would whistle the first bars of *Un Canadien Errant*, just in case it should be Vermette or Cloutier.

Melancholy as it was, the tune had an effect. The first time

I whistled it, a man approached the bush where I was hiding. I slipped out on the other side, hid, and whistled it again. This time he went on his way, either incurious or scared. Another time it was two people and they whistled in reply; but not a Canadian air as the other two would have done. I dived off into the woods, and came back to the tracks by a roundabout route.

Several trains passed. They threw sparks and smoke into the surrounding air; some of them were packed with passengers, and they lit up the forest before disappearing, as they had come, with a rumble. They brought home to me my loneliness.

I came to a railroad crossing. The gatekeeper's house was wrapped in the silence of slumber. I considered knocking at his door and asking for help; it would soon be dawn and what should I do then? I didn't have long to think about it: an enormous police dog rushed out of his kennel, barking furiously and leaping at his chain. He made enough noise to wake the entire neighbourhood, and I waited for somebody to come out; but nothing happened. No light came on in the crossing-keeper's house.

I talked to the dog and gradually he calmed down. I have never been afraid of dogs, and I decided to take this one along as a companion. He might be useful in detecting the presence of strangers in the night. I rolled a piece of bread into a small ball and threw it to him. He jumped at it and swallowed it. At least he wasn't fussy. He was very interested in a second ball, and took it out of my hand. There was still no light or sound from the house, and as I handed him another piece I unsnapped his chain.

When I set off again the dog followed. However I couldn't spare him much of my bread, which was literally all I had to eat, and before I could undo one of my laces to tie him up, he had turned around and scooted back to the house. Perhaps his master had finally woken up and called him back, or perhaps he did not care to take part in my hazardous destiny.

The night was nearly over now, and I had to leave the tracks and start looking for water, food and lodging.

I took the first road that crossed the railway and followed it for several miles, then cut across country. I soon came to a stream flowing with fresh clear water. This was an oasis in the desert; I had been thirsty for a long time, for I had no way of taking any water away with me, except by absorbing as much as possible. Although the night was still very cool, I bathed and rinsed out my undershirt to get rid of the salt.

Much refreshed, I set off again, and soon found myself among orchards. I ate a lot of apples and pears and put some of the best in my jacket as a further provision. I didn't touch my bread, keeping that as a last resort.

Further along the edge of the forest I came upon a little country church, shrouded in ivy and flanked by a small grave-yard; and as the first light of dawn appeared I saw a few scattered houses. It was high time to be getting under cover.

I didn't want to meet early risers, for I intended to choose the time, the place, and the person I should contact. At our escape conference they had said: 'Not in the morning, but at the end of the day. Women in preference to men. Old rather than young. Poor rather than rich. Country people rather than city. Priests and doctors rather than merchants or shopkeepers.'

The village was not awake yet. I came to a small house standing apart from the others. At the back there was a barn with an open door leading to a hayloft with a ladder nailed to the side. The invitation was irresistible. In two seconds I was up the ladder and into the loft. I laid my provisions along the wall where I would not lose them, and spread out my under-shirt to dry. I levelled off the hay for a couch, and trying to remember not to snore, fell instantly asleep.

4

In my sleep I heard a dog barking and the sound of voices. I woke reluctantly, crawled to the opening and looked down. There was a small mongrel dog at the foot of the ladder; he saw me and barked all the more furiously and tried to climb up. A woman's voice called the dog, and added,

'What's wrong with him this morning?'

I could have told her, but refrained. After a minute the voice went away, and through the cracks in the barn wall I saw the woman going to a field nearby. She was holding a small girl by the hand and the dog was following them; once in the field they started gleaning the wheat. That gave me an idea. I climbed down from the loft, and on the barn floor found some wheat stalks tied in bundles. I got several handfuls and climbed back to the loft. With some of the apples I had kept it would keep me going.

I went back to sleep, and when I woke up again, judging by the sun, it was about 1600 hours. The woman was just entering the house. When she came out again she was carrying a big basket on her arm, and set off towards the road. If she was going shopping, it seemed a good opportunity to find some civilian clothes and some food. Much as I disliked the idea of robbing people, there was no alternative if I was to get out of my compromising uniform; but to my dismay I found that the windows were closed by solid shutters and the door well and truly locked.

There was nothing for it but to await the woman's return and see if I could draw on her patriotism or her humanity—preferably before her husband appeared. If they were together, it would be best to avoid them and carry on with my journey.

While waiting, I started thinking out a plan for returning to England. My first idea was to get to the nearest stretch of coast, steal a boat, and sail or row across the Channel. Some Frenchmen did it in 1940, and from where I was at the moment it seemed the logical thing to do. The escape conference, though, had stressed the point of going down through Spain. It seemed silly to go that far when I was still quite close to England. By travelling at night and stealing food, I could probably reach the coast and get hold of a boat, even dressed as I was; while to go south, it was essential to get out of uniform and travel as an ordinary Frenchman, in daytime; and this meant getting help.

Yet the Intelligence officer must have had a good reason for counselling us to go through Spain. It would mean a long trip, and crossing the Pyrenees on foot at the end of it; but to a Commando it should be no great problem. Compared with Canada, France is a small country, but all the same a thousand mile journey is not to be made on foot. I should have to use the railway, and that would need money; but remembering the proverbial generosity of the French towards Canadian soldiers in the 1914 war, that difficulty should not be insoluble. The first and trickiest part was to find a patriotic person and not a *collaborateur*.

Two hours passed, and there was still no sign of the woman. Soon it would be dark, and darkness brings fear. If I scared her she would certainly not help me. Then in the distance I recognized the bark of the little dog. It came racing round the corner and made straight for the barn, running around it several times, looking for a trace of me. Twice it passed within ten feet of me without scenting me. Disappointed, it returned to the house to wait for its mistress. She arrived—alone!

I waited about ten minutes, then went to the door and knocked. She opened it and looked stunned. She had not heard me arrive, nor did the dog bark. I had appeared quite suddenly out of thin air, a bedraggled and unshaven soldier—no wonder she was frightened. With some warning, or more time to think, she might have reacted differently. The dog didn't help by its furious barking. As I explained who I was and showed her my shoulder patches she went quite pale and did not answer.

'I've spent the day in your barn, sleeping,' I said.

She murmured, 'That's why the dog was barking.'

At least she understood what I was saying.

'Can you help me? I'm hungry.'

She shook her head at this.

'I'm alone here and I can't.'

'Do you know anybody who would?'

'Yes, the lady in the big house,' and she pointed across the road. 'Try her.' And with that she went inside and firmly shut the door, leaving me to my own devices. A discouraging start.

5

In the garden of the house she had pointed out, a man was working. As soon as he saw me his eyes became round with amazement; but before he could say anything, a young woman came out of the house and asked what I wanted. She did not seem at all startled; on the contrary she had grasped the situation immediately. She had heard of the Dieppe raid over the radio, and without hesitation she took me to the cellar of a shed at the bottom of the garden. She told me to stay there while she checked whether I had been seen entering her property, and somewhat to my dismay I realized I was a prisoner again. If she were speaking the truth, she should not be away more than two or three minutes; if she were much longer than that I could assume I was being held while somebody was fetching the police or the Germans. I decided to give her five minutes —and it seemed an interminable wait.

It was just about time to try and force the trap-door, when it was opened, and I was allowed up into the shed above. It appeared nobody had seen me, although there were several houses in the vicinity. Moreover she had brought food from the house, and a glass of wine, which, to my unaccustomed taste, was quite bitter.

She told me to get undressed; and Robert the gardener tackled my hobnailed boots. He pulled out the nails and filled the holes with cement, saying that the hobnails would give me away and it was no use trying to find me shoes because they were too scarce. To improve the effect, they smeared them with mud and manure as if they were really a farmer's working boots. The maker's name was ripped off my underwear and I was provided with an old pair of trousers, much too big, and an old faded shirt. The disguise was complete; I was a civilian, and a pretty poor one at that. The only discrepancy was my very short haircut.

Madame Collai, my hostess, had one serious reproach to make.

'Why didn't you come directly here?' she asked me.

'You should put up a sign on your gate,' I replied jokingly, 'saying "Here we greet Allied soldiers". That would prevent mistakes in the future.'

This remark became less funny a little later on.

Mme Collai and Robert decided it was too dangerous for me to stay in the house, so I had to spend the night in a shack in a quarry in the woods. They gave me an empty potato sack, some food, and a plan showing the paths. If anybody questioned me, I was to say that I was picking grass for my rabbits. This seemed to be a national pastime in rural France. My benefactors promised to come out and talk to me after nightfall.

On the way I came to a wall where some fresh notices had been posted. They were interesting, but not of much comfort.

'The death penalty for any member of the population who helps, shelters or fails to reveal the presence of an Allied soldier.'

Perhaps that sign on the gate wasn't such a good idea after all. I was not used to reading threats of death on the walls, and the letters seemed to be written in blood. Mme Collai had three small children.

I dawdled along as a peasant would do. There was no hurry, and I had no wish to draw attention to myself. It was not only my liberty that was at stake, but the lives of several French people as well. Yet now that I had shed my uniform, I felt a new man. I didn't have to hide and I should have much preferred to stay in the fields this pleasant summer evening. Still, the fewer people who saw me the better.

6

So I moved into my new home fervently hoping it would be very temporary. The roof was not too good, but I chose the driest corner in which to make up my bed, brought in some sacks full of leaves for a mattress, and laid the empty sack down for a blanket.

My domestic preparations complete, what could be better than a stroll? The weather was warm, the woods very quiet and pretty. A few pines stood here and there amongst the hardwoods and perfumed the evening air. The old quarry was at the foot of a small slope cut in two by a mossy sunken road. It supplied a red clay used to make pottery, and around the old shack there were piles of broken shards. But the quarry itself had become a pond, with water lilies and green reeds in the shallow reflective waters—a perfect spot for a swim.

Darkness slowly enfolded the forest, and then it began to rain, slowly at first, then faster until it became a steady downpour. A great coolness rose from the earth. For a long time I stood at the door, watching the rain; the corner where I had made my bed was the only place that remained dry. The waiting seemed endless, and strange ideas began to run through my head. Eventually, tired of my own thoughts, I set off through the rain to meet my new friends, and sheltered under a big tree near the road.

When at last they came it was by another route, and their two shadows appeared behind me, beside the shack. They had brought more clothes and food with them, and while I ate they asked me what I wanted to do. My first idea, to make my way back to the Channel, they regarded as madness. It would be virtually impossible, they said, to approach the coast, and even if one succeeded, every boat would be under lock and key. The Channel was hardly to be rowed across, and anyway it was constantly patrolled.

My second choice, to go through the Pyrenees and into Spain and so make my way to Gibraltar, they considered much more promising. Admittedly it would mean travelling in broad daylight, by train, but they did not seem to notice that I had a strange accent for a Frenchman.

We talked on into the night and finally we agreed to meet again next day. That night was very restful; I had no particular worries, and the lack of comfort did not bother me.

Next morning the rain had stopped and the day dawned fair. To my surprise, Robert appeared, but he was simply bringing me soap, a towel, a razor and, most precious of all, a map of France. It had been torn out of a geography book belonging to one of Mme Collai's children, and was not very detailed; but it was a lot better than nothing.

7

Punctually at nine o'clock Mme Collai was at our rendezvous, armed with more clothes, nearer my size, which she told me she had stolen from a rag-picker's garret—what an amazing woman! The trousers must have once belonged to a postman, for they had a red stripe down the sides, but at least they almost fitted me. There was also a new shirt, a clean coat and a beret, and some provisions in a small jute sack. A lot of French workers, she said, would be travelling with something similar.

Nor was that all. She gave me most of the money she had at hand, and bread coupons, without which one could neither eat in a restaurant nor buy bread at a bakery. Finally she briefed me on how to travel, and where the demarcation line ran that separated the German-occupied zone in the north and the unoccupied zone in the south. It was just south of Poitiers, and I should have to cross it on foot, as I had no papers. On foot and unseen.

When everything was settled, she accompanied me to the railway station of Bourgtheroulde (Eure) and I asked for a third class ticket for Poitiers. This was the first time I had tried to pass myself off as a Frenchman; and standing there at the wicket with my guide watching me, I felt as if everybody were listening to my accent, and that it was perfectly obvious I was a foreigner.

The clerk asked me whether I was entitled to a reduction. This was something I had not been prepared for, and for a moment I was flummoxed; but then, just as I was about to retreat, he gave me a ticket.

'That'll be 190 francs, m'sieur.'

I gave him a 500 franc note, grabbed my change and fled as if I had just had to deal with Hitler himself.

It was ten o'clock and the train was not due till twelve, so I followed Mme Collai to a deserted road not too far from the station. We went through the whole procedure again and she tried to foresee every possible situation I might have to handle. Then it was time to go. She and Robert had been magnificent, and I owed them more than I could ever repay, but it was a relief to be on the move again. I was eager to start my long journey back to England.

CHAPTER FIVE

Through Occupied France

1

WHEN the train pulled in it was already packed. But the people who wanted to get on pushed and shoved until they were inside, and as I was standing in front of a carriage door I just hung on to my little sack and got swept in with them.

Conditions inside were unbelievable. It was hardly possible to breathe. An assortment of boxes, sacks, and old worn-out valises tied up with string were stacked up in the corridor, among bags of potatoes, baskets of vegetables and a variety of small livestock. The quest for food seemed to be the only reason people travelled.

At last the train struggled into motion, and I waved a discreet good-bye to Mme Collai and tried to put into this simple gesture all my thankfulness for her help and courage.

Further along the corridor there was a German soldier with all his equipment, including his rifle. For an instant our eyes met and my heart raced. However, he looked quite unperturbed, and I told myself that, to him, I must look like just another Frenchman. At Elbeuf I had to change, and so did he. I did not dare ask for any information, and stayed on the platform with many of the other passengers. At each exit a member of the *Feldgendarmerie* was inspecting the papers of the people leaving the station. I was safe for the moment—unless they decided to check the papers of those on the platforms too. But some time I should have to leave the sanctuary of a railway station, and I should certainly get caught unless I got off where there were no German guards, as at Bourgtheroulde. From now on, though, I would be on a main line, and there was likely to be more checking rather than less. It seemed to be part of the routine of travelling, for everyone took it as a matter of course. If it had been a spot check, the travellers would have been surprised and few would have been ready with their papers. It was an anxious hour, and I felt that everyone, including the guards, was staring at me. Like an ostrich, I moved behind a column where I could not see them.

When the train arrived, it was less crowded than the previous one, and the luggage, although there was plenty of it, was more conventional. Everything went well until we got to Le Mans; as soon as the train halted there German soldiers came on demanding papers. It was no time for lingering, and I was off the train in a hurry, although I tried to make my departure look natural. Mercifully, there was only a ticket-collector at the exit; no Germans, no papers needed. In a moment I was through and out in the street.

2

The main thing was to get clear of the town before the curfew, and I started marching with no idea where I was heading. After a while the houses got sparser. On the edge of town there was some kind of checkpoint, manned by *gendarmes*; but they did not seem interested in pedestrians, only in cars.

Three men came along, talking together. I fell into step behind them, and when we came up to the kiosk I was on the outside and abreast of them as if I were part of the group. The men inside the kiosk didn't even glance up.

All the same, it wasn't until I was two miles away and in open country that I began to calm down. A farmer was working alone in a field by the roadside, and I decided to ask him for hospitality.

I explained who and what I was, but he was distinctly suspicious, and I could hardly blame him. We were far from Dieppe here; and although I spoke French he knew that the Germans were in the habit of sending out *agents provocateurs* to incriminate patriotic Frenchmen. He didn't actually refuse, but he attempted to check on my story. I answered his questions as best I could, and at last he reluctantly consented to take me to his home. When we got there, he went indoors leaving me in the yard, and through the window I could see him talking to his wife. Although they brought me some food eventually, they didn't ask me indoors. They answered my questions on French ways, ration tickets and so forth, but only very grudgingly.

My quarters for the night consisted of a small stable, already occupied by a colt, with a bundle of straw for a bed; and when the farmer left me, he bolted the door on the outside. His mangy dog was tied up just beyond where I stood. In case the farmer was making sure of me until he could get in touch with the Germans, I set about arranging one or two exits. A small boarded-up window responded to treatment; and I also managed to slip back the bolt on the door by means of a bent straw. All the same, I spent a restless night, waking up five or six times imagining that the dog had barked and the Germans were at the door.

In the morning the farmer gave me my marching orders.

'You can have something to eat, but then you must leave immediately.'

In talking to me he had been using the French familiar *tu* that a lot of country people use even with strangers.

Once again with this gruff and suspicious pair, their actions belied their words. Not only did the woman give me a large piece of bread and a bowl of coffee, but she sent me on my way with a bacon sandwich and some hard-boiled eggs.

3

It was Sunday morning, the city streets were empty, and there was no train until nightfall. A long day stretched ahead of me, and I couldn't think where to pass the time without risk of being picked up either by the *gendarmes* or by a German patrol.

I felt helpless and conspicuous; and yet, among the people in their Sunday black strolling home from Mass, or gathering in increasing numbers at a street market a little further on, there must be some who would be prepared to help me. But how to find them? To outward appearances there was nothing to distinguish those who might be sympathetic from those who might betray me. Perhaps if I eavesdropped on their conversation, I might get a clue to their loyalties.

In the crowd at the market I spotted a man pushing a bicycle. He tipped his cap to a woman and helped her with her shopping basket. I followed them and picked up a few remarks on the stupidity of the French authorities who were giving away material to the Boche, and on the possible meaning of the Dieppe raid.

At a crossroads they separated. The man was about to climb on his bike when I approached him and explained briefly who I was and what I wanted from him. He was justifiably surprised, particularly as he had just been talking about the raid. He offered to take me to a friend of his who had a restaurant nearby. There was a lot of whispering with the owner of the establishment, and I was invited to sit on the terrace. The place was packed, for a bicycle race was due to pass the door at any moment. Everybody seemed to know everybody else, and all about the racers, and each had his pet champion. One asked me my opinion. I answered by smiling and raising my shoulders.

'Pas causant, le pote!' (Not very talkative, this bloke).

As soon as the race had gone through, the terrace was invaded by a crowd of men and five took up their stance around me. They were looking at me oddly, and I realized they were regular customers and I had pinched their table!

They were workmen from a nearby factory, and the Germans were forcing them to work on Sunday. They tried to draw me into their conversation, but I was too scared of giving myself away to get involved.

After they had left, the proprietress came over and offered me a glass of cognac. She seemed a bit suspicious still; and when I asked her how much I owed her, she asked me for meat tickets. I suppose that my air of incomprehension as I fumbled with the coupons reassured her. She picked up my money, counted it, and asked if I had any more.

'No, that's the lot.'

At this she took a 500 franc note out of the till and handing it to me, wished me good luck and a good trip. Such spontaneous generosity was humbling.

I spent the afternoon asleep in the fields, and in the evening I walked slowly back to the station, in good time for the train to Tours.

I had no trouble getting into the station, or on to the train, which was far from crowded, probably because it was Sunday. In my compartment there was one other couple. The young woman offered me an apple, and I was glad to accept it. The train had hardly started when she went to sleep, followed shortly afterwards by her husband. As I had nothing to do and nothing to read, I soon followed suit.

I was woken by a tall uniformed man standing in the doorway. My heart rose to my mouth; this was it, he was going to ask me for my papers! It took me several seconds to grasp that he only wanted to check my ticket.

At Tours, while changing trains, I helped a woman who was heavily loaded with luggage. I found I wasn't half so scared of the public as I had been. She was bound for Poitiers, and I questioned her closely. We had an hour to wait; and during that time I discovered that she lived near the demarcation line and had crossed into the free zone several times. She gave me invaluable information on the distance from Poitiers to the line, its direction, and various ways of crossing it. She seemed to take me for a French prisoner who had escaped from Germany and was trying to get home or at least into the free zone. I didn't let on who I was. However, as we got on board the train, I must have said or done something strange, because she closed up tight. I thanked her for her help, and found myself a seat in another compartment.

We arrived at Poitiers during the night and all the passengers left the station, although the curfew was still in force. I lay down on a bench and went to sleep. At six o'clock I walked out without being noticed; I didn't even have to give up my ticket, as there was nobody on duty.

I knew that I had to make for Limoges, and it was with a lively step that I set off into the country. I was not very far from the free zone, and if I could once get across the line there would be no Germans, and travel should be easier. It lay only about five hours ahead, but I still had to be careful. The woman on the train had told me that capture was all too easy even after crossing the line. I was confident the crossing itself would be no problem, because, having been a hunter and a soldier, I felt I should be able to negotiate it successfully. The next sunrise, I thought, should see me safely in the free zone.

I stepped off the road to take stock and form a plan of action. I had enough information for the time being. I knew that it was definitely easier to cross after dark; in the meantime, I had to make my approach with caution. I watched the road for over an hour. Most of the traffic consisted of farm carts, and peasants on bicycles or on foot. There were also a few cars, mostly, as far as I could judge, local people going about their business, though one or two had luggage and a number of passengers.

The people who were least likely to be challenged were the local peasants. Most of them would be known, though not necessarily to a roving patrol. The more I resembled them the better. My clothes should pass all right; but my little sack might suggest that I was on the move; so I emptied it, folded it up, and slipped it under my shirt. It might come in useful later on.

My provisions would last me for about twenty-four hours only, and this was an inducement to push on, although I could manage for several days without food if I had to. I could get fruit and vegetables from the fields, but I had to have something more solid than that if I were to keep my strength up.

The bottle of water was half full, but it was beginning to smell. The best thing was to leave the cork off and carry it in my side coat pocket as I had seen French workers do with their wine bottles. I ate part of my food and stuffed the rest into my pockets. I should have to get something to drink later on, marching would be thirsty work under the hot sun. What a fool I had been not to have filled my bottle back in Poitiers.

I set off along the road, and when, after a mile or so, I saw a woman in front of a farmhouse, I stopped and asked her for a drink. She gave me a glass of wine. I was supposed to be a Frenchman, so I could hardly refuse to drink it, but the bitter taste only made me thirstier. I asked her how far it was to the line, and she told me that it was eighteen kilometres, adding that I shouldn't go any further than the crossroads at Fleure or I might get into trouble. Realizing that she had guessed my intentions, I left in a hurry without asking her to fill my water bottle.

Once I was out of her sight, it occurred to me that I had panicked unnecessarily. She was probably quite used to travellers asking questions, and she had certainly given me that warning gratuitously. I cursed myself for behaving like a nervous idiot.

Back on the road, I covered about three miles very quickly. I kept a watch for cars coming from either direction, and if there was time I would nip into the fields. Occasionally, on bends, I would get caught out, and then the only thing to do was to keep on marching. I was able to fill my water bottle, and wash and shave, in a murky little stream in a nearby wood. That made me look a bit more presentable and less Bohemian; and after an hour or two's steady marching I came to the crossroads at Fleure.

This was the danger zone; probably everyone, except perhaps the locals, was liable to be called on to show his papers. Best to wait for dark. If, in the meantime, I could glean any further information, so much the better.

5

Across the way was a smithy with a cottage attached. I knocked and asked for a glass of water. When I asked for a second, the young woman looked at me quizzically, as much as to say, 'There's an odd Frenchman for you, drinking water like that.'

'You from Poitiers?' she asked.

'Yes, and it's quite hot on the road.'

'You'd better not go on, it's dangerous.' This was the second time I had been warned. I nodded, and said:

'Would you mind filling my water bottle?'

'Not at all,' she said; and then:

'Why don't you come in and sit down until nightfall?'

No invitation could have been more welcome. Once indoors, we continued chatting, and I decided I could trust her with the truth. For a moment she stood speechless; then she flew next door to the forge to fetch her husband.

He made me repeat what I had told her, and then he grabbed my hand and shook it as if he would never let go. His initial disbelief was understandable. We had landed on 19 August, and it was still only the 24th. In five days I had been involved in the raid, been taken prisoner, escaped, found civilian clothes, and travelled about 250 miles.

He wanted to know all about the raid and the coming invasion; this, for the majority of Frenchmen and women, was the burning question—when? Unfortunately I could not tell him exactly.

But I had burning questions of my own to ask him. I outlined my plan for crossing into the free zone and making for Spain on foot across the Pyrenees. He approved, saying that others had succeeded—but only to end up in a Spanish gaol. This was something that would have to be looked into later. For the moment, the main thing was crossing the line. To my astonishment, the blacksmith immediately offered to take me across himself. He had done it many times before. He seemed to be something of a smuggler of human beings, this unusual blacksmith. All the same I refused the offer. I reckoned I could find my own way across and it would merely be subjecting him to a needless risk.

He drew me a map of the surrounding country, showing the guard posts, and warned me about the roving patrols which were usually accompanied by police dogs. On the border itself, he told me, the Germans kept watch from a platform in a high tree to the left of the road. Once over the line I should be past the guard posts, French and German, which were on the main road; but I still shouldn't be entirely safe. The French police of the Vichy Government were always on the look-out for people who might have crossed the line.

Thus carefully briefed, I was all ready to leave when a cart came along, driven by an old peasant accompanied by his grandchild. He had come to pick up some machinery that the blacksmith had made. Immediately the two of them went into a huddle, with an occasional searching glance in my direction. At last they came back, and the blacksmith announced that his friend had agreed to take me part of the way.

I was delighted. Not only would I be less conspicuous than marching alone along the road, but I would be sure of the place where I had to leave the road and take to the fields. I thanked the blacksmith profusely for his hospitality and his help. Once again he seized my hand, saying,

'I trust you. Now, here's another point. When you get to Lussac-les-Châteaux, on the Limoges road, go to the "Hôtel de la Gare" and ask for Père La Classe. He's a friend of mine. Bon voyage.'

The cart rumbled into motion. The old man sat silent, absorbed in his thoughts. We had the road to ourselves. At length, he stopped and pointed.

'There's the ditch. Follow it as far as that field of Jerusalem artichokes. Take cover and don't move before dark. You'll be in full view of the Boche. When it's dark enough, make for that wood over yonder.'

It was his longest, indeed his only, speech; yet I was sure he knew all about me. Without another word he jerked his horse into life, and I made for the ditch. It was quite deep enough to hide me, and I crouched down in it, listening to the clump, clump as the horse went on its way and very much aware that I was on my own once more. Now, however, I knew exactly what I had to do.

6

I had plenty of time before nightfall, and I spent part of it examining and memorizing the route I had to take. I had no intention of being caught at this stage if I could help it.

When it grew dark and I was free to go, I closed my eyes and counted slowly to 200. When I opened them my night vision had improved, and so I set off with infinite care across the fields towards the forest. I had plenty of time; there was no need to blunder into a trap. Once among the trees I lay down and listened.

There was no sound, and in a short while the moon appeared. This was fine; it would give me my direction. I orientated myself; I had to keep the moon ahead of me and just to my left, not forgetting to allow for its movement across my front.

Going deeper into the forest, I sat down to eat the sandwich the blacksmith's wife had given me. There was no noise except the gentle rustle of the leaves; no clink of weapons, no footsteps, no dogs barking. I sniffed the air to try and detect the smell of cigarettes. I had proved to my soldiers that when they smoked on guard duty I could smell it a good distance away. Sloppy enemy soldiers could well reveal their presence to me by smoking.

Satisfied, I set off again, stopping frequently to listen, avoiding paths and trails. It was slow progress, but I didn't mind that; I had all night.

At last the forest opened up and there were fields in front of me. I crossed them, pushing through the hedges and ditches that marked their boundaries. Several times I had to make detours to avoid farm houses. I moved silently, and the dogs did not stir. In the rich orchards I made free of the pears and peaches.

Now I should be coming up to the railway that separated the zones. There it was in front of me! It glinted in the dark. It ran right across my path from east to west. I could cross it; I was dying to. Instead I forced myself to pause.

The track was just the place for patrols to lie in wait. They could sit in the bushes and keep a watch in both directions; and I wasn't going to oblige them. I inspected each bush on my side for several hundred yards; then I watched the other side—looking, listening, sniffing.

Everything was quiet; there was no movement, sound or smell.

I came back to the centre of the area that I had reconnoitred, jumped over the fence, sprinted across the ballast, skimmed over the opposite fence and dived into the bushes. When I stopped to listen there was only one sound and that was my heart thumping. I had made it!

CHAPTER SIX

A Temporary Refuge

1

I WAS inside the free zone, and my spirits soared. I quickly found the road and started marching south at a good pace. I wanted to be well clear before daylight. My heart was singing; I hadn't a care in the world.

I woke up to the fact that a soldier was standing in the road in front of me about fifty yards away.

His voice snapped, 'Halt!'

I could not tell whether he was French or German and had no intention of finding out. I could have kicked myself for being so careless! My mind was racing: how was I going to get myself out of this spot?

Without faltering in my step I started to march backwards. I heard the click of his rifle bolt, then, less assured, 'Halt' again, followed by some phrase I couldn't make out. I must have gained ten paces in my backward march, but now it was high time to get out. I did a quick jump to the right into the ditch and out into the bushes. None too soon, as it transpired, because he had started firing, and, for a man without a definite mark, he wasn't doing too badly. The bullets were whistling all round me.

Someone was yelling: that would be the guards turning out to search for me. Well, they would have a long search; I was scooting along in the ditch as fast as I could go.

When I reached a spot where some tall trees hung over the road, making a patch of deep shadow, I turned up my collar, put my hands in my pockets and, looking the other way so that my face wouldn't show, crossed the road slowly and silently and slipped into cover on the opposite side.

The undergrowth was so thick that I had trouble making headway. Brambles scratched my hands and tore at my clothes; I had to use my knife to hack a way through. Every now and again I listened; there was not a sound behind me. I was getting tired now, and when I came across a path, I followed it. Then I thought—that's just where they'll be expecting me; so I slipped back into the undergrowth.

A little later I remembered another menace—dogs! Though I hadn't heard any barking, they could have been brought in to pick up my trail by the road. I had better keep moving.

After a time I came to a field of artichokes, leading away from the road. This was just what I needed. It offered good cover, and since the rows were about two feet apart, allowed me to move fast. But the artichokes soon came to an end, and ahead of me lay nothing but open fields. I was about 500 yards from the road.

Back at Witley, our base camp in England, I had been quite a useful performer in the four mile cross-country run. Then it was running shoes; now it was heavy boots, but that was only a minor handicap in the circumstances. I rolled up my coat and tucked it under my left arm, and was off at a long distance pace, watching all the time for movement on my right.

At last I reached a small copse and slowed down. I must have been five miles away from the post, but it was too early to stop yet. When I reached the road again I kept walking alongside it for about another four miles.

I came to a cosy haystack set 100 yards back from the road: just what I needed! I bedded down, warm and safe for the remainder of the night.

2

I was woken up about 0800 hours by the sound of a truck rumbling past. Although I had slept for only a few hours, I felt quite refreshed. I ate my last sandwich; it was a bit dry, and I was out of water again. The sun was shining and things looked bright. I even began to imagine I could hear a British aircraft coming in to land in the field and take me back to England.

Lighthearted as I felt, when I set off along the road again, I was careful to take cover whenever I heard a car coming. However, I must have got too absorbed in my thoughts, because one I never heard until it was too late. It was a private car, and it slowed down as it came up with me. Was this because of the bend in the road, or were the occupants interested in my doings? All I could do was stand my ground, but be ready to run on the instant.

I turned to face the oncoming car. There were two people in it, one of them a woman. Hardly the police. I walked on again as casually as I could, hands in pockets. When the car was right alongside, the woman wound down her window and the driver leant across her.

'Are you going to Lussac-les-Châteaux?'

'Yes, it's on my way.'

'Would you like a lift?'

They looked honest, straightforward people, so I thanked them and climbed into the back. What a bit of luck, I thought; and yet, a prisoner on the run soon learns never to relax. I had nearly learnt that lesson the hard way.

The woman started chatting to me, but I could see the man watching me in his rear-view mirror. I found this inhibited conversation, particularly as she kept asking me questions about myself. However, we soon arrived in Lussac, and the car came to a halt in front of a garage. They were stopping there; and as I thanked them, the man asked:

'Would you be going to the Hôtel de la Gare?'

'Not particularly,' I replied, 'unless the cooking is good.'

'The cooking is exceptionally good; you should try it,' and he pointed the road out.

Now how the devil did he know that was where I was bound for? There was only one person who could have told him, and that was the blacksmith from Fleure. So either he had been through there that morning, or he had been called up on the phone. He was definitely on the look-out for me.

And then there was the old man who turned up so conveniently with his cart. He must have been briefed, too. The

79

only person who could have set all this in motion was the blacksmith. Suddenly I felt as if a whole conspiracy had been formed to help me on my way, and a wave of gratitude towards all these brave and friendly folk swept over me. I had been incredibly fortunate.

3

The Hôtel de la Gare was fairly typical of its kind. Under a shabby sign, the door opened directly into a room which did duty as village café, hotel entrance and reception. It was full of people, mostly country folk, and pulsing with noise and laughter. A few glanced at me as I came in, but incuriously. I found a seat by the wall and surveyed my surroundings.

There were two people serving the customers: a very pretty young woman who, I noticed, was wearing a wedding ring, and an old man who might be her father. He was about sixty, with square shoulders and a slight stoop. His hair was almost white, and his hands were coarse and weathered, more like a farmer's than a hotel-keeper's. They went with his clothes, the grey flannel shirt, the ancient baggy trousers, and the felt carpet slippers. This must be Père La Classe whom the blacksmith had mentioned.

When, shortly afterwards everybody left, apparently to catch a train, I saw my chance. Stepping to the door at the back, which led into the kitchen, I beckoned to the woman who was cooking at the range. I took her to be Père's wife, a big woman with a mass of grey hair and an expression on her face which was far from friendly. Deliberately picking up a heavy poker from the side of the stove, she came towards me. If I hadn't had good reason to believe these people to be pro-Allies, I should have taken to my heels; but when I mentioned the blacksmith of Fleure, she looked a little less as if she intended to land me one with her poker.

Instead, she went into conference with her husband and daughter, who were observing the confrontation from the far side of the stove. Finally the old man came over, shook me by the hand and welcomed me to his house. A place was set in the back room and they brought me good coffee with milk and sugar and fresh bread and butter—in marked contrast to the black bread and roasted acorns served in the café.

While I was wolfing it down, they asked me all sorts of questions; and as I told them my story, they began to smile, and finally burst out laughing. I asked them what the joke was.

Apparently I had arrived just after the *gendarmes*, who were checking everyone's papers, had gone. The garage man, Andrault, who had given me a lift, had phoned to say I was coming, but they had got it wrong and understood that I was an official of some kind. The red-striped trousers confirmed this impression— which explained why they had appeared so suspicious at first. The hotelier, whose name was Vayer, was an active member of the Resistance, and so had reason to be cautious. On a previous occasion they had taken in three British airmen.

We all had a good laugh at the misunderstanding, and as we laughed, Andrault, the early morning driver and owner of the garage, arrived to check that I had found the hotel. He was reassured at seeing us all in such a merry mood.

I was given a small room upstairs. From the window I could step out on to an adjoining roof, and by scrambling over a wall and down into the yard of the warehouse next door, could escape into the street. I found this arrangement conducive to peace of mind; the room was very clean, quiet and cool; I lay down on the bed and was instantly asleep.

4

When I went down for supper, the Vayers' son-in-law, Jean, who was an engine driver, had arrived. He had been to a meeting of the local Resistance at which they had planned my future. I was to remain at the hotel, as a cousin of Jean's who was breaking his journey to Marseilles. In the meantime they would get me false identity papers and try and find a way to get me back to England. The three airmen had been picked up by a Lysander after staying there for three weeks.

A few days later, M Milet, the director of a local mill, fetched me in his car to have my picture taken for identity papers. Cars were very scarce in France at this time, but he was entitled to one for business purposes. Like most of the others, it ran on charcoal, to burn which it had a furnace lashed to one side of the bonnet and a heater for the extraction of gas from the charcoal on the other. The resulting performance was feeble, but it worked.

The portrait which the photographer at Châtellerault produced shook me; the hunted look on my face was exactly that of a gaolbird on the run. The next day I got my identity card. It was made out in my own name; but my birthplace was given as the neighbouring village of Queaux, and I had a job locally. I could not help wondering whether my supposed employer would give me a good reference!

Now that I was a bona fide Frenchman I didn't mind being seen about so much, but I was told to stay out of the public eye as much as possible. I was still quite a risk, both to myself and to all those who were trying to help me. Through M Andrault, I was taken to meet a M Louis Pradet, who lived in Limoges, and who was reputed to have organized the escape of the three airmen. He promised to try and work the same miracle for me, but he didn't sound too hopeful.

When the weather was fine I worked in the garden, and at mealtimes I helped with the dishes. I tried to keep busy in order not to think too much about the enforced waiting. Jean, my 'cousin', was keen on angling and we often went out with rod and line, or to swim in the river a few miles away.

I had a scare one night when *gendarmes* knocked the hotel up at two o'clock in the morning. I took to the roof; however, they were looking not for me but for a Jewish woman and her seven-year-old son. Their cries as the police dragged them away were terrible to hear. There was a camp near Poitiers packed with Jewish families who had tried to cross into the free zone, for the Vichy police were arresting French citizens and handing them over to the Germans. As I climbed back into my room, it was with the thought that other people were in a far worse plight than I, and this helped me to resign myself to waiting.

As one week became two, and two became three, I was getting more and more edgy. All I wanted was to get back to England and my battalion, and I was becoming desperate enough to try anything. I knew everyone was doing their utmost to help me, and they tried to cheer me up with news of fresh leads and hopeful contacts; but there was nothing definite, and the uncertainty and the waiting frayed my temper. I had to get out.

CHAPTER SEVEN

South to the Sea

1

ONE day two friends of La Classe arrived, on the run from the Gestapo. Some of their comrades had been arrested, and it was time they disappeared. Their names were Gaston Chapron and Nicolas Saurin, both from Poitiers, and they wanted to reach England and join General de Gaulle.

Since we were all trying to go the same way it seemed sensible to join forces, and so it was agreed. My hosts could hardly fail to notice my joy at leaving them, though I tried not to show it too much; but they understood that I couldn't stay with them indefinitely, as much on their account as on my own.

The morning of our departure I awoke early. It was October now, and it was still dark outside, without a trace of dawn. I dressed quickly, picked up my little case, and went downstairs. The whole family were up and waiting in the small dining room.

We had breakfast together; Père La Classe let no one but himself make the toast and pour the coffee, as a sign of our friendship. The men did not speak much; all they had to say had been said yesterday when making the plan. But the women contributed all the anxious, unhelpful suggestions that a mother or a sister would make to a son or a brother. To them, I really was '*le cousin Lucien*'.

When I picked up my things both women kissed me good-bye, and they were crying. Then Père La Classe grasped my hand, his rugged palm compressing all his feelings into the gesture. Canadian I might be, but he said:

'Il faut *que je t'embrasse.'*

This was the first time that I had been kissed by a man, and I felt his prickly two-day-old beard rubbing my cheek. Knowing enough about French customs by now, I was half-expecting this and would have missed it for the rest of my life if he had not done it.

It was now Jean's turn and this was briefer. I moved towards the door through which I had come five weeks ago. A new adventure was about to begin, or the same one was being resumed; but I was a different man now. I had papers and could pass as a Frenchman; I had money in my pocket, and could travel alone and unafraid should it become necessary.

2

Outside, it was very cold. Andrault had promised to drive me to a station some fifteen miles away to catch the early train, so as to avoid any of the local people seeing me leave. But his car wouldn't start and it was a good ten minutes before he succeeded in getting it going. Luckily we had allowed plenty of time, and we reached the station as the train drew in.

Andrault shoved me into a crowded compartment, and told me that Saurin was to join me. I was a bit worried as we were supposed to meet on the platform. It was still dark as the train pulled out, and there was no sign of him, but at the next station he came into the compartment. I had seen no sign of Chapron, but judging from the events so far, he could well be somewhere else on the train.

Saurin did not approach me, or betray in any way that we knew each other, so I took my cue from him. Thus, as complete strangers, we travelled as far as Limoges. On arrival I followed Saurin off the train and into the main hall of the station, and soon Chapron joined us, coming not from the platform but from the town. He must have come into Limoges the night before. Now, at last, we felt free to recognize each other openly and travel together. Of my two companions, Chapron seemed to be the leader and gave the orders.

Half an hour later we were on our way to Marseilles. Saurin

was soon deep in conversation with our fellow travellers; but despite my identity papers, I preferred to keep silent. I didn't feel confident enough regarding French customs, and I was self-conscious about my accent.

In any case I was far too excited at the prospect of escape even to notice the countryside we were passing through. 'England, England,' the wheels said over and over again as they carried us all that day and all the following night, south and east through the highlands of Cantal and Lozère into the Languedoc, and so, at last, to Marseilles.

It was six o'clock in the morning, and the street-cleaners were busy washing down the cobbles with water from hydrants which, I reflected, had this been Canada, would soon be lost under a foot of snow.

Marseilles, bustling with life and noise and smells, was my first large French city; but of all the smells that assailed my nostrils, the most interesting was the sea. I had caught a glimpse of it as we came out of the station, and I imagined that all I had to do was find a ship and sail for England. I was soon to discover that a passage to England could not be booked at the first travel agent.

3

My companions quickly set about establishing contacts. We visited several cafés and houses, and long conversations took place resulting in messages, both verbal and written, being left for mysterious third parties. Chapron and Saurin told me nothing, and it was safer that way. I was content to leave these preliminaries to them. Something might come of it all, in time.

At Lussac, we had been told that there was still an American Consul at Marseilles. This had since been confirmed by several other people, and I was convinced that he held the key to our escape. My friends agreed; but when I suggested that we should simply walk in, tell him who we were, and ask him to get us out, they were utterly opposed to the idea. All we should get, they said, would be a curt refusal. I argued, and finally they agreed to give it a try. If it did not work, at least we should be no worse off.

We found the Consulate without difficulty, and at the reception desk I announced in English that I was an American citizen and would like an audience with the Consul.

He kept us waiting fifteen minutes, but then he saw us and I told him my story. If I had expected him to be surprised, I was disappointed. He listened without any expression, and when I had finished, asked me a lot of questions in English. As soon as he realized that I was Canadian, not American, the interview was over.

'The United States is a neutral country,' he said, 'There's nothing I can do for you.'

I was dumbfounded. I couldn't argue with him, for there was nothing to say, so, bitterly disappointed, we took our leave.

We went back to La Cannebière, the main avenue in Marseilles, and ordered a good lunch to soften the blow. Personally, I simply refused to believe it; but whichever way we looked at it, the situation was not too bright. In the opinion of Saurin and Chapron, it was their presence that caused the Consul to refuse to have anything to do with us, and I had to admit that they were probably right.

It was a painful realization; we had sworn to keep together, and yet already the force of events was breaking us apart. We discussed it endlessly; but both of them insisted that I tried again, alone.

4

The Consul saw me at once, and I gave him no opportunity to speak first.

'You're American and I'm Canadian. Does that frontier really make so much difference?'

He looked slightly taken aback. 'Where are your French friends?'

'I left them in a café.'

He seemed to consider for a moment. 'Go to this address. There you'll find a doctor. Tell him you've a sore throat and a sore right foot. Go at once; and don't tell your friends. Good-bye and good luck.' And that was all.

I found the house easily. There was a brass plate by the door, so there couldn't be any mistake. I rang the bell, and the door was answered by an elderly maid in a black dress and white apron, who showed me into the waiting room. Two women were there already. When my turn came I went into the surgery.

'Doctor, I have a sore throat and a sore right foot.'

'Who sent you?'

'The American Consul.'

He nodded. 'Good. Come this way.'

He led me through a door at the back of his office, through the dining room, and into a bedroom beyond. This was his son's room, but for the time being I was to treat it as my own. There were clothes in the cupboards; and if there was anything else I needed, all I had to do was ring for the maid. The doctor excused himself for leaving me alone. It was like being a long-awaited guest.

I didn't have to ring for the maid. No sooner had I taken off my coat and was undoing my heavy boots than she came in to ask whether I would like anything to eat. At the same time, she brought pyjamas, bedroom slippers and a dressing gown, and showed me my private bathroom. She then took away my own clothes for cleaning and mending.

This was my first real bath since arriving in France, and a great luxury it was. After it I chose a book from the shelves and lay down on the bed to read. I was woken by the maid coming in to tell me that her mistress had come home and was waiting for me to have afternoon tea with her.

This in itself was odd; but no odder than the fact that my hostess spoke perfect English, although, to all appearances, she was an educated and intelligent Frenchwoman. The doctor, her husband, she told me, was of Greek origin, and she herself had spent a long time in England. So we chatted over the teacups and the cakes for an hour or so; and when at length she excused herself, it was with an invitation to join them for dinner. In the meantime, here was another armful of books to keep me going.

The doctor turned out to be a great conversationalist, learned and interesting. He was quite tall, handsome, with a shock of white hair, and had served in the French army. His opinion of the Germans was made amply clear, and although he didn't say much about it, I gathered that he was doing his best to inconvenience them in any way open to him.

It was a delightful and civilized evening; but I wasn't sorry to be allowed to go off to bed quite early. I had been rather short of sleep.

For the next few days I stayed in my room reading most of the time, coming out only for meals, which I shared with my host and hostess. They kept me company as much as they could during the day, to help prevent the time from dragging too much; and at night heavy curtains were drawn over the windows and carefully checked to make sure that we were not visible from outside. I felt at once both a guest and a prisoner, and was soon longing to be once more on my way. I didn't have long to wait.

One evening, about a week after my arrival, I was introduced to a friend of the doctor's known as Pat.* He spoke both French and English fluently, seemed to know Canada well, and quizzed me thoroughly on my knowledge of Quebec Province and Montreal. I must have passed this oral examination; because at the end of it he announced that I should be leaving within forty-eight hours. This news dumbfounded me. I had reckoned I had landed in good hands; but after the long weeks of waiting at Lussac, I was resigned to a similar delay here. This was wonderful news. I told him of my two French companions and where they could be found, and he promised to do what he could for them.

* His organization was later to be betrayed by a man known as *Roger le Légionnaire* (see p. 182).

CHAPTER EIGHT

The Last Lap

1

PAT was at the station to meet me. I said farewell to the good doctor, very conscious that I had incurred yet another debt of gratitude, and found myself ushered into a compartment full of men. They did not look like normal travellers; one in particular was a ferocious-looking character, and I wondered what I had landed myself in for this time.

When Pat started to introduce me to the others, *in English*, I seriously began to wonder what crazy company I had fallen into. Then the penny dropped: all these chaps were in exactly the same situation as I was. Several of them were English, and the tough-looking one turned out to be a Scot who had been taken prisoner at Dunkirk, and had been on the run virtually ever since—two years or more.

It made me realize how incredibly lucky I had been. I had been in German hands for no more than a day and a half, and all the French people I had met worked hard to help me. As a result, after only six weeks, I was on my way to England —or almost. Lucky, indeed, but undoubtedly being able to speak the language had helped.

After some time we all had to change trains, and caught a railcar bound for Perpignan. The track followed the coast for part of the way, and the sight of the sea filled us with a wild exhilaration.

2

At Perpignan we separated into groups, each led by a different guide from Pat's network, and set off by tram for Canet-Plage almost on the Spanish border.

Speaking French put me in the odd position of being half an escaped prisoner, like the others, and half a part-time recruit to the network. For instance I stayed at the local hotel with the guides and took my meals with them. The proprietor was a member of the network, and as the season was over and the hotel was empty, we had the run of the place.

A ship was supposed to be coming from Gibraltar to fetch us, so there was nothing to do but wait for it to arrive. The rest of the party, sixty-five all told, were herded into a cottage on the beach, and each evening after dark we took food down to them in baskets. Conditions in the cottage were unimaginable; the building consisted of three small rooms, and was supposed to be uninhabited, so no lights could be shown at night and nobody was allowed near a window in the daytime.

There wasn't even enough room for everybody to lie down, so there were four men on each bed, four more underneath; two men on the table, two underneath, and so on. Every available flat space was occupied, and in depth!

After three days of this 'seaside holiday', Pat announced that the boat was due the following night. Since the Royal Navy was looking after us, it could hardly be anything smaller than a destroyer; the 'Med', particularly along the Spanish coast, should be pretty safe from German interference, and at thirty knots or so, our troubles should soon be over. So we thought.

3

At midnight we were given our instructions, and at one o'clock in the morning we slipped out of the cottage and headed for the rendezvous in single file, to wait for the boat from the Royal Navy. The night air was cool, and once we got away from the houses and into the open country, we ran as wild as colts.

It really was good to stretch our legs along the smooth, sandy beach.

When we reached the place, we settled down on the sand to watch and wait. We were soon shivering. For the next three hours we tried to make out in the darkness the shape of small boats heading inshore; but for all our imaginings, no boat came that night, and before dawn broke we traipsed back to the cottage, with the prospect of another twenty-four hours in our prison without bars. We were all deeply depressed, and the agents' assurances that it was all laid on for the following night were not enough to cheer us up.

We slept for much of the day, and again, that night, we returned to the beach to watch for a darker shape to appear out of the darkness. But once again we were disappointed.

We had found out that the boat was to come three nights in a row, so the next night was our last chance. This time we spread out to cover a good mile of beach, in case the boat did not come to the exact spot. Nothing happened.

Pat promised to contact The Rock again to find out what had gone wrong. He didn't disclose how he would do it, and we knew better than to ask him; but one of his agents was away for twenty-four hours and we reckoned he must have gone back to Marseilles, possibly to make radio contact.

He returned with the news that the boat had indeed come to the beach three nights running but had not been able to find us, and had therefore turned back. Now it was to try once more, for the very last time.

Again we spread out along the beach, every eye straining into the darkness. After about fifteen minutes I caught a glimpse of something a bit blacker than its surroundings. It seemed to be real; but I forced myself to close my eyes for ten seconds. When I opened them again, the dark spot was still there and it was definitely growing bigger. It was a boat, all right, and I was not the only one who had seen it; our guides were by the water's edge. The whistle which was the signal to regroup was passed along the line; and at that moment I spotted a second boat making for the shore. This was it, at last – unless it was a coastal patrol.

Our first sight of the boats themselves sobered us; they were no bigger than dinghies, with room for about two people besides the oarsman. This didn't prevent the guides cramming eight people on board each, and I found I was expected to stand up! I was enough of a sailor to know that in cockleshells as small as these one must sit down if one is to avoid capsizing it; and so I very gingerly bent down to hang on to the side – to find the tips of my fingers were in the water. There was about an inch of freeboard.

Fortunately the sea was calm, but we held our breath all the same, until, after a few minutes, we began to make out a dark shape against the sky. As soon as we came alongside everybody grabbed the rail, and we scrambled aboard, and the skiff set off for another load.

It was obvious at once that this was no destroyer. It did not require an inspection to tell us that our deliverer was a small trawler; the smell told us as much. Not that it mattered, just so long as it would get us to The Rock.

It took about an hour to ferry everyone out. Then the boats were hoisted aboard, the engine rumbled into life, and we headed out to sea.

4

At daybreak the coast of Spain and the Pyrenees beyond lay on our starboard hand. We might well have been marching over those mountains, with a good chance of rotting in a Spanish gaol at the end of it, had it not been for this slow and shabby little vessel.

Her captain and crew were all Polish; and she was so small that there was no room for us below, and not even enough room on deck for everyone to lie down at the same time. With a blanket each, we were left to make out as best we could. Luckily the weather was fine and mild.

Later that morning the Captain addressed us in his excellent English. We were on our way to Gib, he told us, but well off-shore, as the Spanish were not allowing any foreign ship to enter their coastal zone. If we were approached by another ship or by aircraft, we were to vanish, either below decks or under the upturned boats or the fishing nets. The trawler carried all her fishing gear, and if we were challenged, she must appear to be going about her normal occupation.

All this was straightforward enough; the bad news came at the end. Because of the delay in picking us up, they had been at sea much longer than had been foreseen, and they were running short of both food and water. We should therefore be rationed to three cups of water per man per day, three biscuits and a tin of sardines. Moreover as soon as we were out of sight of Spain, we had to repaint the ship!

While we were busy altering the appearance of the hull and upperworks, the crew changed the sails for others of different colours. Presumably we were as short of fuel as of everything else, for we hoisted a sail whenever there was any breeze.

Our progress was so slow that the skipper signalled for a naval ship to pick us up, but the reply from Gib was negative; and so rations were cut to one cup of water and one biscuit a day. The sardines had all gone, and now the water-barrel was taken below and locked up.

Next day some of us got only half a biscuit and half a cup of water. After establishing that the correct amount had been given out by the crew for distribution, two commando corporals and I got together; we agreed that a group of Scottish soldiers had been fiddling the rations, and we decided to keep an eye on them.

That afternoon the ship was stopped so that the sailors could finish painting on the waterline, and we were allowed to swim. The heat being intense, there were clothes all over the deck in a matter of seconds. The swimmers had taken a flying leap over the side, and the non-swimmers were busy finding ropes to hang on to. The water did our dehydrated bodies a power of good.

By the end of that day we were really suffering from hunger and thirst. It being three days since we had had anything resembling a meal, our thirst was constant. We tried to assuage it by soaking our arms in sea water, and pouring bucketfuls over ourselves. At least it cooled us off. Meanwhile our little vessel pushed on at her maximum speed of six knots, and we let the time slip idly by, watching the empty sea and thinking of food and drink.

The next day, when ration time came around, we were watching. I had formed a group of NCOs and asked the OC Troops—an RAF officer with the smallest idea of discipline—to form up the men in line. There was trouble almost at once, some of the men trying to get back into the queue after getting their ration. Before we could do anything, the Captain came out of the wheelhouse with a pistol at his belt and two sailors at his side. He walked over to the trouble-makers and told them shortly that if they did not leave the queue, the sailors would throw them overboard. The only thing he omitted to say was whether he would shoot them first. After that the rations were fairly distributed, and there was no more cheating.

That afternoon, after our daily swim, we saw smoke to port. We were soon in our hiding places, and there we stayed, cramped and stifled, for what seemed like ages, until at last it disappeared over the horizon and we were allowed out. According to the Captain, it was a Spanish ship making for Africa.

The following day an Italian aircraft came over to inspect us. Again we performed our vanishing trick, while the sailors stood about and waved. It circled us for some time before flying off, apparently satisfied that we were just an innocent fishing vessel.

That night was our fifth on board, and the time dragged on endlessly. To encourage us, the Captain told us that we should be in Gib the next day.

We were abruptly woken at three o'clock in the morning by two loud explosions, one to starboard followed by a closer one to port. The engine revs dropped back. A shape grew out of the dark and we heard a bellow from a loudspeaker—in English.

'What ship are you?'

We could almost feel the pressure on the triggers of guns ready to blast us to pieces. Then our Captain shouted back: 'His Majesty's Ship, *Sea Lion*!'

We could hardly believe our ears. We had speculated endlessly about the ship and her allegiance; but none of us, in our wildest fancies, had imagined that the smelly old trawler with her crew of Polish ruffians was a member of the Royal Navy!

At daybreak Gibraltar soared over the horizon, a mighty

sight and one most comforting to us; but we were still not quite out of the wood. As the ship tacked round to enter the harbour, we were ordered into hiding once again. This seemed the final indignity, arriving at a British port, but the Captain explained that The Rock was under constant watch from spies, and if they saw us on board, the ship's disguise would be compromised. We must not even be seen going ashore from her; so as we docked, longshoremen made a kind of passage out of packing-cases between a warehouse and the ship's side, and as we got ready to run ashore, a destroyer passed close to our vessel and blocked off the view from across the basin. We dashed between the packing-cases and into the shed, where army trucks were waiting for us. As soon as we were in, the flaps were closed and we were away. We may have felt like refugees or criminals, but we were back on British soil and that was all that mattered.

6

Five days later I was flown to London, to be met at the airport by Intelligence, who showed a most flattering interest in my adventures. For the next seven days I was subjected to almost continuous interrogation by officers of every service and every nationality. In the middle of this massive session, I was ordered to report to HQ, Combined Operations. There I was introduced to Lord Louis Mountbatten; and, worst ordeal of all, with only a commando corporal for support, found myself on a floodlit stage facing the top brass of all the Allied Services—including Douglas Fairbanks Jnr.

Then, back to Intelligence. They were particularly interested in the details of my journey through France; and after several periods of intensive questioning, they came at last to the point: would I be interested in going back into France to do work similar to that of Pat O'Leary, the man who had organized our escape in *Sea Lion*?

My answer was a very definite no. I had had my fill of being lost behind the enemy lines, and was in no mood to resume that tense, hunted life which the photograph taken in Châtellerault had so vividly revealed.

The officer who made the suggestion did not seem unduly surprised at my refusal.

'If you ever change your mind, you've only to contact us. We'll be glad to hear from you.'

Never, old chap, I said to myself.

I was allowed to leave at last, to return to my unit. My only desire was to take up the threads of my old job and get on with the war. The last thing I intended to do was to get involved with an organization like the British Intelligence Service; but as I was to discover, there are more ways of fighting an enemy than shooting him.

PART TWO

Back to Occupied France

CHAPTER ONE

On Probation

1

Six months went by. For four of them I was in North Africa, attached to the British First Army as an observer; and then, with that much more battle experience, I was posted back to my battalion. During this period, General MacNaughton, GOC Canadian Army, nominated me for a commission—but I refused. I had applied for one two years previously and been rejected; now it was my turn to be awkward.

It was mid-1943. The Allied armies had completed the re-conquest of North Africa and were soon to cross the Mediterranean, and—apart from our eight hours on the beaches of Dieppe—set foot for the first time in three years on the mainland of Europe. This was the moment that every Allied soldier, and most of the inhabitants of the occupied countries, certainly the ones I had met on my travels through France the previous year, were waiting for. I should have been part of the coming invasion myself if it had not been for the arrival, fresh from Canada, of a new platoon commander.

He knew it all, this little gentleman; and after a week or two of his airs and ignorance, I found myself remembering the officer in Intelligence and his invitation. I had never known his name; but I did know that he was a major wearing a Military Cross and had only one arm, having lost the other at Dunkirk, where he was captured. Despite this inconvenience, he had succeeded in parting company with his German hosts and escaping to England. In direct disobedience to my tiresome new platoon commander, I asked Canadian Intelligence to put me in touch with the one-armed major; and in due course I was granted an interview with him.

This took place in St James's Park. The major was quite young, very dapper, with piercing eyes and a neat moustache. He told me his name was Langley (in fact it was Windham-Wright, but I only discovered that much later) and he was perfectly friendly. The friendliness, however, as I soon realized, was neither here nor there; and if I had thought of it at the time, there was a certain incongruity in that first meeting: sitting on a park bench in the summer sunshine, discussing in the most offhand and prosaic terms the possibility of my undertaking an assignment of blood-chilling loneliness and risk.

'You do realize, Sergeant-Major,' said Major Langley, 'what you are letting yourself in for if you're accepted, don't you?'

I said that I did. I had, after all, experienced the work at first hand from the receiving end, so to speak. The major nodded.

'And if things go wrong, and you're caught?'

'I suppose I shall be shot.'

'Eventually, yes; but only after the Gestapo have finished with you.'

'I understand,' I said, and suddenly it seemed as if the day had grown chilly.

'And there will be nothing we can do for you. Nothing. As far as we are concerned, you will have ceased to exist.'

'Isn't that a bit rough?'

'It's a rough game, Sergeant-Major. Well?'

'I've made up my mind. I'm ready to go.'

'Not so fast. First of all, we have to decide whether you can be of use to us.'

2

Three days later I was instructed to report to Canadian Military Headquarters in London, and was granted a fortnight's leave; but this, I quickly found out, was so that the major and I could continue our al fresco conversations. If it rained, as it did on occasions, we retired to his club, or to a rented hotel room. He gave me a Whitehall telephone number—though I never succeeded in contacting him on it—and he asked me a great many questions, some of them very strange ones indeed. Gradually I came to realize that my whole past life, every hole and corner of it, was being brought out and closely scrutinized. It was an uncomfortable sensation. Nor did it stop with the past.

One evening, with time on my hands, I nipped down to Godalming to look up an old girl-friend. We spent a lively and enjoyable twenty-four hours together, and I returned to London. At our next meeting, Major Langley said:

'Where were you yesterday? I phoned your room and there was no reply.'

'I was in Godalming. I was stationed there.'

'Seeing a girl?'

I nodded. 'Her name and address?'

This was going too far.

'Wait a minute, Major,' I protested. 'This is a personal matter.'

'With us,' Major Langley said curtly, 'there is no such thing as a "personal matter". I want to know who she is, where she lives, and how you spent your time.'

It was then I realized that he knew already, so there wasn't much point in trying to protect the girl, or disguise the fact that we had spent quite a lot of our time together in bed. There certainly were no 'personal matters' in this enterprise.

Other unaccountable things happened during those weeks. Strangers would come up to me in pubs, press drinks on me, and then try to pump me; and once I was picked up by the police on some trumped-up charge. On another occasion, it was the MPs accusing me of having a forged pass. They overdid it, I got angry and insisted on laying a charge against them. When I mentioned it to Langley, he told me to forget it. Like everything else that happened during that fortnight, I realized it was a put-up job designed to test my reactions. It made me even more on my guard; but I could still be caught out.

One morning I was told to report to the Free French HQ and ask for a certain captain. Langley was there and introduced us, then strolled away, leaving us talking. The French captain asked me a number of loaded questions, and then, staring at my chest, snapped:

'And may I ask why you are wearing a medal to which you are not entitled?'

This really got my goat and I lost my temper.

'If you weren't in uniform,' I said, 'I'd fill you in'—and a lot more on the same lines. I was seething. The major returned from examining the pictures on the far wall.

'Cool down, Lucien. I just wanted to find out how good your French is. Now I know.' He turned to the captain. 'What do you think?'

'The accent could be that of central France—say the Nivernais. I suggest his background be constructed accordingly.'

When we left, he grinned and shook my hand. No hard feelings; but I felt a fool, all the same.

3

Towards the end of the fortnight the major gave me my let-out. The unit needed a man of my experience to train the youngsters, and in any case, I was old enough to quit active service. There would be no disgrace in this; on the contrary, I had the MM to prove that I had done my bit. He summed up:

'You'd be far more sensible to return to your unit.' Did he mean that I had failed in some way, and was not wanted? Or was he simply giving me a final opportunity to have second thoughts? Already I was getting used to looking for a trap. But I had no intention of backing down now, and I said so forcibly.

'Fine,' said Major Langley, 'Glad to have you with us.'

There was not even a handshake; just this casual sentence, 'Glad to have you with us.'

I was 'in'.

CHAPTER TWO

Training for a Life of Crime

1

THE next day, we went to fetch my things from Canadian HQ. As I was given civilian clothing, I packed my uniforms in my military bags; then we drove to the Canadian Records Office. When my bags and rifle were registered, the major casually reached over, picked up the check and slipped it into his pocket. It was as good as saying that there was very little chance of my collecting my gear in person. In fact, I was about to cease to exist at all, for my name was posted on the 'Q' list of people about whom no information was available. There was only one stage after that, the 'X' list, and those on it were dead. The major and I had a ceremonial drink to celebrate my impending demise.

My next meeting with him was in the street. He was accompanied by a young man, about twenty-two years old, athletically built and with a determined jaw. We went to a room that had been reserved for us. The major introduced us and said:

'You two get acquainted, hold nothing back, nothing is secret between you.' Then he left us together.

Raymond La Brosse, my new room-mate, was also a French-speaking Canadian. He had lived in Ottawa all his life before joining the army, and had been a sergeant with the Signal Corps attached to the Canadian Artillery. We had quite a number of things in common.

He was reticent at first; but when I told him that I had been on the Dieppe raid and of my escape, he opened up. He had been contacted by MI9, probably because he was a good radio operator, spoke good French, and was a fearless and determined young man.

He had parachuted into France with his chief in order to form a network to recover Allied troops. His chief, whom I was to meet later, was a flamboyant character who had to do everything in a big way, regardless of the risks involved. Inevitably the Gestapo got on to them. They caught Ray, his chief, and a lot of others.

Ray succeeded in escaping from the Gestapo, only to find himself with a faulty wireless set, no cipher, no money and twenty-seven airmen on his hands. Most people would have got out of there fast, and alone, saying to themselves:

'These airmen are not risking their necks as I am; if they're caught they'll only be sent to a prisoner of war camp.'

But Ray did not succumb to that argument. He dragged his party of escaped prisoners through France and across the Pyrenees into Spain. From Madrid he was flown to London.

The office left us strictly alone for a week, and then the major asked us whether we would like to work together as a team.

We had spent a lot of time analysing the failure of the previous network, and Ray knew my views on security. In the light of that, and my Dieppe escapade, he accepted me as chief, while he would be my assistant and radio operator. This suited me. Although I had discovered that he was one of the untidiest people I had ever come across, I admired his courage in not having pulled out of France by himself; it suggested that in a tight situation he would be reliable. So I accepted him, despite his disorderliness—after all we weren't getting married! —but I insisted on two conditions. Ray was to have a code of his own; and his wireless set, as well as his code, was to be tested in the British Isles.

This was my first step as chief of a network. It seemed to me essential to be able to inform base of any imminent disaster, and so avoid a repetition of Ray's mishap.

In going back to France, he was running a greater risk than I. He would be known to the Gestapo, and they would have his description, if not his photograph. In addition, because of his youth and physique, he would always be in danger of being picked out for forced labour in Germany, as happened to so many young Frenchmen.

I would be safer on that score, not only because I intended to increase my age on my identity papers, but also because I was growing a moustache and would wear neutral glasses. Both of these could be taken off quickly if necessary, a better dodge than growing a beard, which takes time, and putting on dark glasses, which tend to be conspicuous.

2

Our work started in earnest. Although we still occupied our room when in London, we were often away on various courses. For example, parachuting. Ray, being a qualified parachutist, only did a few jumps to keep his hand in, but I had to start from scratch.

I was therefore sent to a parachuting school in company with a lot of other 'civilians'. Everyone had a different accent, and we realized that we were all prospective agents, earmarked for different countries. We knew each other's first names—and nothing else at all.

Of course, parachuting is very easy and a lot of fun. Any instructor will assure you of this. At least we had to agree that falling out of an aeroplane sounded easy enough. Our instructors had a sense of humour. If a trainee hesitated in choosing a chute, there would be one of those Simon Legrees on hand to say:

'Choose any one you like; they're all guaranteed, you know; and if it doesn't open, you can always come back and get another.'

Any further hesitation was sure to bring forth:

'I don't think you like the way it's been folded, so you'd better fold it yourself.' And with that he would rip the pack open.

We had been shown how to fold a chute, and although the WAAF parachute packer did not hold much authority by rank, she held our attention. We watched her very carefully. Later, we did fold our own packs—and they always opened!

At first we jumped from 600 feet; but this steadily became lower and lower with each jump until we were almost scraping the tree-tops. Our chutes were hardly open before we hit the ground. This was necessary for the kind of jump we were to do; the less time in the air the better.

After landing we had to hide our chutes. Another fellow and I dug up a bush, put our chutes underneath, scattered the extra earth in a carrot patch and let the instructors go on searching. The farmer probably wondered why that particular bush did not grow well!

3

From parachute jumping we turned to security, which, of all disciplines, is the most vital to an agent. Quite accidentally, I committed a serious breach of security myself, and one which nearly got me sacked. I was interviewed on my experiences in France by a reporter; and the story was passed by the censor for publication—but without a picture of me, as it was thought the enemy might put two and two together. However, when it was passed to the local paper in Montreal, they simply sent up to my folks for a photo and used that. When I showed the cutting to the major, he nearly had apoplexy, and I was only allowed to continue at my own risk. (Come to think of it, who else was at risk at any time?)

One important aspect of security which we had to consider was the question of women. Too many agents owed their capture and death to becoming involved with a woman who had, perhaps, become jealous and then given them away. There was only one safe rule, our lecturer said, 'Have nothing to do with them.' General dismay. He gave us an alternative: 'If you must have a woman, don't tell her about your work.' Not being a monk or a eunuch, I took due note.

From security we were put on to police work, which included following a suspect. Then we played it the other way round, ourselves being followed. This part was a lot of fun. I had done some police work before and succeeded in losing my pursuers three times in four hours. They gave up.

We learnt pistol-shooting on a range beneath Baker Street station. In a room fifteen feet wide by thirty feet long stood ten men. When an instructor called your number and a target number, you pulled your gun from its shoulder holster, pushed aside the other instructor who had been asking you to light his cigarette, went into a crouch, and weaving in between the others, got six shots off in pairs. The main object was to get the first two shots off fast. With practice we became red-hot at this, and our pistols could hardly be seen being drawn; a flash, and they were blazing. We also practised disarming a man threatening us with a pistol.

Ray and I had chosen two pistols apiece, a light one and a heavy one, to take with us to France. We should not normally go around with pistols on our persons, since it would be courting trouble, and there would be few occasions to use them. Our wits would be our chief weapons; but if we should get into a tight corner it might be possible to shoot our way out.

On the course we also learnt a number of non-police skills; these included forcing door and suitcase locks, and even opening a safe. As time went on, we gradually acquired all the qualifications of a professional burglar or hoodlum.

4

Ray went up to Scotland to try out his wireless set. He came back after two days, and reported that it was not working. The major had said that I was being unduly fussy when I insisted on testing the set; now it seemed I had been right. I did not let him forget it.

A few days later we tried again, and this time both reception and transmission were good, but Ray was not satisfied with his ciphering and deciphering. We used telegraphic wording jumbled according to a prearranged key. Each cipherer had a different key. Therefore nobody but the London office and the cipherer himself could read it. It needed intense concentration; even to construct a simple message could take forty-five minutes, working fast. If you changed one letter for another, the message was still readable, but if you skipped a letter or put in one too many, the result was gibberish.

It was all-important for a cipherer to be proficient, and, of course, there was no question of putting the code down on paper. The key changed with each message, to make things a little harder for the enemy decipherer. The only help you had was squared paper, which a lot of people used in France, and which would not, therefore, be out of place if it was found in your pockets; but as soon as a message had been noted, it had to be destroyed. The simplest way was to tear it in small pieces and flush it down a WC. Burning was less reliable, since it left ashes that could be read.

5

The story that the office had made up for me was partially true, and sounded plausible. I repeated it to Ray, to the major, to Mr Johnson, our QM, who supplied us with everything including French suits of clothes, to the police, and to myself at night. It was in my mind when I went to sleep, and soon I came to believe it myself. I was Lucien Desbiens, born in Amiens, rue des Trois Cailloux, Administrator of Funeral Enterprises, now living at 40 rue Violet, Paris XVe. I was an associate of Barbier et Besse, morticians, of 65 avenue de Bretagne, Paris.

During the security course we had been subjected, with our consent and help, since it was a necessity with our job, to a personality change. It was a two-part process. First, we were quite simply dehumanized. To begin with it was not painful; but after a while we realized that our superiors considered us as 'out of this world', that is, dead men already. We had been expecting this all along, but when it happened it hurt.

Secondly, we were gradually being depersonalized. Obviously it was not possible to stop being Lucien Dumais, just like that, as I was continually meeting people I knew; but as I tried to assume my new personality and live with it, my contact with my old, true self began to grow weaker; and, of course, once I stepped out of England, I would cease to be Lucien Dumais and become Lucien J. Desbiens, the undertaker from Amiens, not just in name but in person, and would have to act and live and think as he would, and completely forget about the old Lucien, the commando Sergeant-Major from Montreal.

All this left me with a strange feeling of not having existed before; and sometimes I seemed to be searching for myself; I longed to become my old self, and could not. At the same time, my new personality was something I wasn't yet sure of; it was something made up, that had never existed before, and felt as if it only half-belonged to me, like a suit of clothes I had borrowed.

Until one has worn oneself into a new personality, which takes time, as one has to form new habits, one has this terrible blank, lost feeling. For, when all is said and done, one loves oneself, one's own personality; and no matter how bad it is, one still does not want to part with it.

Nevertheless, if I were ever caught and interrogated, my disguise would be checked and rechecked; and no matter how good it was, eventually it would be proved untrue. Eventually one would make some tiny slip and give oneself away. I knew this, and made up my mind that I would answer freely up to the point when the questioning became serious. Then I would shut up and refuse even to give my name. Preferably I wouldn't get caught.

CHAPTER THREE

Cross-Channel

1

THE last details were tied up. We were given a number code, micro-photographed on to cards so tiny you needed a magnifying-glass to read them. We had a long session with the navy, who told us exactly what they would be able to do for us, and we planned a number of pick-ups by sea which seemed feasible. All the essential information was written down, and that was also put on microfilm.

At last we were ready to go. In our pockets and distributed about our persons were demob papers, old metro tickets, French money, two small compasses, road maps, tear-gas fountain pens, wire metal saws (hidden in our trouser turn-ups), escape ropes made up into the soles of house slippers, and so on.

We were each given a money belt. I gave Ray a quarter of a million francs and kept half a million. I would need more cash than he as I would be paying all operating expenses. The major said:

'Don't be stingy, spend as much as you see fit; we can always let you have more if you need it. Keep no accounts, they're dangerous; we're not interested in money, but in results.'

His last instructions were our contact address in Paris, a hair-dressing shop in the rue des Capucines, and the pass-word. As to how we were to go, and when, that was another matter. The first plan, which I favoured, was for us to be taken by sea and put ashore on some unfrequented bit of coast; and when that was cancelled, we were given the choice of parachuting into France, or being landed by aircraft. I preferred the latter and said so. All that remained was to wait for a suitable moon —or so it seemed. Every morning we rang the office, to be told 'Ring back tomorrow.' Then it came. 'Stand by. You will be picked up by car at 1830 hours.'

It was a long day. We tried to pass the time pleasantly, but suddenly the future seemed very close. The next twenty-four hours would see us either lost among the Paris crowds, or captured by the Germans. They had been on the reception committee often enough in the past. One careless word by one of our contacts on the other side would be enough for a *collaborateur* to make the necessary deductions, and we would be welcomed by a few platoons of German troops.

Oppressed by thoughts like these, we got through the day as best we could. We couldn't even enjoy a drink, aware that we were going to need all our wits, and a clear head.

2

Right on the dot of 1830, two staff cars, driven by astonishingly beautiful women, swept up to the door. All our officers were there, and they looked after the luggage. We were the VIPs.

The one-armed major had become a Lieutenant-Colonel, and we congratulated him sincerely. His was a thankless job. He worried constantly about his agents, and it must have been nerve-racking to watch them disappear into the night sky, one after the other, and know that it was unlikely that he would ever set eyes on any of them again.

After an hour's drive, we came to an airfield. It was dark, but we could see the RAF guards on the gate. They checked the cars' and the drivers' papers but not the passengers'.

Apparently we had plenty of time on our hands, and so we made ourselves comfortable in the Nissen hut they took us to and which seemed to be kept for this purpose. Five or six RAF officers had come in and one of them was introduced as our 'driver'. Drinks were handed round.

The girls took off their jackets and went to a corner where

there was a small stove and proceeded to cook us ham and eggs —a rarity in England just then—and we knew we were being offered the condemned man's last meal.

3

About 2300 hours our driver looked at his watch and said:
'Let's have a last one.' We did.

The cars took us across the airfield to a parked Lysander. Two sentries had been keeping it company; they were dismissed. We climbed aboard and stowed our luggage in the rear cockpit. As the 'Lizzie' was only a two-seater, this didn't leave much room for Ray and me.

Having stashed everything as best we could, we climbed down again and joined the group of officers waiting beside the aircraft. The colonel said:
'Let's hear from you soon.'

The two girls accompanied us back to the plane and we kissed them good-bye passionately. It was a symbolic leave-taking: we were kissing not only these girls but all our girl-friends and the world that we knew. Then the hatch was closed, the engine revved up, and we were away, bound for central France, where a committee was to receive us. Over the French coast we ran into fog; I heard the pilot talking over the wireless and then he banked around. I had my compass and checked the course: we were heading back to England.

Over the intercom the pilot told us that the fog was too thick for him to land. I had a suspicion that something else was wrong, possibly at our destination, and that London had been warned and had ordered the plane back. How could the pilot tell he could not land when he was still an hour away?

As we came back over the coast of France we saw a shadow behind us, and I reported it to the pilot. He said:
'Keep a sharp watch, it's probably a night fighter.'

Soon it was back on our right and coming in fast; our pilot must have been watching because as I called:
'Left, left, quickly!' our plane was already on a wing-tip. We saw a burst of gunfire but to our left and astern. It was all

over in a flash. We travelled too slowly and turned too fast for that fighter, especially at night when he could hardly see us.

The pilot got back on his course and we recovered our breath. We were not bothered again.

A very dejected group, we landed back at the airfield, climbed into the cars and returned to London.

4

Again we started ringing up every morning, and at last, after ten days of waiting, the message came. The procedure was exactly the same as the first time, even to the girls kissing us good-bye, only this time two other planes took off with us. They were also Lizzies. We had not seen the other passengers.

We went down as far as Poitiers. And there was the airfield with its flarepath lit. We circled while the first aircraft put on its landing lights and started its approach. In the beam we could see people running on the ground below.

As soon as the aircraft stopped rolling, our pilot straightened out to go in. As we made our approach, the radio crackled and a voice yelled:

'Don't land! Don't land! It's too soft. I'm bogged down.'

Reluctantly we climbed away and circled round with the third plane following. There was nothing we could do. Again we headed back to England.

Over Calais or Cherbourg the Jerries opened up with ack-ack. This gave us a jolt. The first shot was above us and the second underneath and so close that we felt the lift from the explosion. The pilot pushed the nose down and gave her the gun. There were three more shots, but behind us. Then we were clear.

We heard later that the first aircraft had finally been pulled out of the mud by a team of horses just before daylight, and had landed in England on the last drops of fuel.

For us the waiting started again. We were very depressed and wondered whether we should ever get to France; we were beginning to believe there was a jinx on us. Every time an operation was cancelled we sneered. Finally I told the colonel we would go by chute. He said there was an operation on in two days' time; if that failed we would be sent in by parachute.

5

Three aircraft were once again taking part, and we were in the lead plane. As soon as our pilot saw the flares he started to lose height. He made one tight circuit, then began his approach. The other two clung close to us, in perfect formation. As the wheels touched we started to open the hatch; much too soon! Hurriedly we closed it to prevent ourselves from being blown out. As the aircraft stopped rolling, we opened it again. We both drew our guns, just in case we had the wrong reception committee.

A civilian appeared out of the darkness and yelled at the pilot; everything seemed to be all right.

Ray was out in a flash with his radio. The ground crew came running up. Ray put his radio between his feet and when one of the crew reached for it, he got:

'*Laissez ça tranquille!*'

I passed down our gear, and the ground crew ran to the edge of the field with it. It was difficult to get going after being cramped up for hours. I kept my briefcase in my hand and jumped down. Immediately three men who had been waiting by the tailplane, climbed aboard. I never thought they could all get in; but they did, and closed the hatch. Even without luggage it would be a tight squeeze.

Ray and I ran to the edge of the field where our gear had been taken. One of the crew had a flashlight and we were able to make sure that everything was there. This was no time to be losing things.

There were four other incoming passengers, and the ground crew were keeping each group separate, not only, perhaps, in order to keep their luggage apart, but also to prevent one group from meeting any of the others. We had now truly entered a world where such knowledge might mean death.

There were five men in charge of each planeload, plus the

leader of the operation who was keeping an eye on things while he talked to the leading pilot. In addition there were three men on the flarepath.

The aircraft flashed their landing lights, turned, and taxied to the other end of the field, where some flashlights were blinking. They swung into wind; the leading aircraft put on its lights, the others did the same, and then they were racing down the field in perfect formation. They had been on the ground for barely five minutes. This was due to the efficiency of the receiving crew, every one of whom knew his job perfectly.

It had been a well-planned and well-executed operation. As the engine notes of the three aircraft faded, we knew that now, after all the weeks of postponement, we were on our own.

CHAPTER FOUR

First Contacts

1

In a small clearing 300 yards from the field, three trucks were waiting. Our leader identified his, and we climbed into the back with the crew and were away immediately.

After half a mile or so, it slowed down, and two of the crew jumped off and disappeared into a farmhouse. Several miles further on the truck turned off into a farmyard and was driven straight into a shed. The door was shut behind us, the engine switched off, and we were told to stay where we were and be quiet.

The silence lasted several minutes. Then at last someone hissed at us from a dark doorway leading into the house, and we went in and were made welcome. Ray was still hanging on to his radio and I to my briefcase.

There was another listening session. People were looking in all directions from the darkened windows. This group was wary and I liked that.

Drinks were poured out, and we saluted one another. Questions were thrown at us, about the coming invasion, about what was going on in England, and especially about whether the Allies were really strong. There was some talk about the Dieppe raid, but I did not reveal that I had been on it. As far as they were concerned we were just two Frenchmen.

I congratulated them on the smoothness of our landing operation; they said:

'We have a very good chief, you will meet him in the morning.'

'It will be a pleasure,' I said.

We were still talking when daylight came and the farm awoke to its daily life. Sleep had been out of the question, not only because of the excitement, but also because we were to move on as soon as possible.

We were eating a much-needed breakfast when in came an elderly man who was introduced as the chief. We shook hands, and I told him:

'My sincere congratulations on your excellent work and that of your men.'

No names were exchanged. We had met by necessity, and each would go his way unknown to the others.

At nine o'clock that morning we left in the same truck. We discovered later that the chief was director of a sugar factory at Chauny, in the Aisne region; now he took us to an empty part of his house, which stood across the road from the plant. He assured us that we were perfectly safe as he had told his staff we were police from the hated Vichy government. He occasionally did have such police in his house in connection with the control of his factory's production; it was certain that we should be shunned.

There was only one anxiety, which occurred to both Ray and me. Our host fed us from the workers' canteen; supposing some patriot, believing us to be Vichy cops, put rat poison in our food!

We stayed two days with the director, during which time we had long discussions. He desperately wanted to know when the invasion would take place, so that he could fight the Boche openly, and was most disappointed that I knew nothing about the matter. I promised to tell him if I ever found out, but there was not a chance of my learning anything about it. Certainly I had seen preparations for it taking shape in England, but as to the date, anybody's guess was as good as mine.

2

Word came that, everything being quiet, we could proceed to Paris. We had been under the chief's orders since landing and would be until we got there. He gave us an address to fall back on, in case our contacts failed us. Hôtel des Jeuneurs, rue des Jeuneurs, Paris.

Ray and I travelled by train in the same coach, but behaved as if we were strangers. On arriving at the Gare du Nord he led me to the left-luggage counter, where we left everything but my briefcase and the wireless set. This was the first time I had ever been to Paris, but the occasion was not at all as I had imagined it!

In the rue des Capucines we found the hairdresser's shop, and while Ray waited outside I went in and asked for Madame Georges. My heart was beating fast; this was where my mission began, and I had been preparing for it for a long time.

A young woman came forward and said she was Madame Georges. I gave the password and she answered correctly. Now everything was up to me. I was British Intelligence Service, taking over a network.

Without more ado, the young woman put on a coat and came out. We went to a park to talk, and it reminded me that, not long ago, I had been having talks in parks, but in London, not Paris. I noticed Ray sitting down a little distance away. I told the young woman:

'I have just come in from London; they told me to contact you.'

'I'm very glad to see you. I hope you can help me.'

'That's why I'm here.'

'Good. I hope you have some money, and a way to send back "parcels".' (A parcel is an evacuee; it must be rewrapped and stamped; that is, given other clothes and false identity papers.)

'Money's no problem. I've all we need.'

'You're lucky. I've had to borrow from everybody I know to get my parcels to Spain. I'm at the end of my tether.'

'Don't worry, I'll get things straightened out.'

It seemed that she had been sending her parcels south to Spain, but many of them had failed to get across the border, and of those that did, the great majority had ended up in Spanish gaols. She was already in debt to the tune of 40,000 francs; but that, at least, could be put right at once.

Marguerite Carrier who worked in the security section for Shelburn

9 Louisette Lorre, the author's liaison agent, who was later killed when serving with the French army in Indo-China

10 The beach in Brittany from which escaping airmen were successfully embarked, although it was surrounded by enemy listening and observation posts

11 The small *camion* of Francois Kérambrun which was used to ferry 'parcels' to the meeting point prior to embarkation

12 The rendezvous house above the beach after it was burned down by the Germans in 1944

'If only you had come before,' she said, and there were tears in her eyes. 'We've had so much trouble.'

'By the way,' I said, 'you can call me Armand.'

'And you can call me Christine. I'll phone Suzanne, my assistant, and get her to come over. You can stay at her house in Rueil-Malmaison.'

We returned to the shop, where Christine went straight to the telephone. Suzanne worked as a nurse at the Clinique des Bleuets close by, and soon arrived. After a lot of whispering at the back of the shop, she came forward to take us to her house.

Once outside, I signalled Ray to join us, as we were to travel together, and introduced him as Claude. These false names were necessary, and we changed them every time we met new people. We never showed our papers to any of our contacts, even though they were false. The change of name would throw off any investigator who checked on us by name; but it meant that we always had to remember which one we had used with each group.

On our way to Rueil, we came to a river, and Suzanne told me with a touch of pride that we were crossing the Seine. I had heard a lot about the Seine, and looked hard. I am afraid I was not as impressed as I should have been. Ray noticed my disappointment, and grinned. We were used to the St Lawrence and this river did not stand comparison with it.

Suzanne lived in a two-storey house; she was a tenant and occupied the second floor. The owner lived downstairs. As soon as we walked in, Ray and I inspected the building for escape routes. We must have seemed quite strange to Suzanne, and very impolite. Still, we had not come from London to be polite, or to care what people thought of us. Precautions are useless only until you have failed to take a necessary one, and then it is too late.

My army experience had taught me that leading men is easy; pushing them forward from the rear, ignoring the fact that they think you are scared, takes a different sort of courage. Dash is a great thing, but it has put more commanders out of action than any other form of conduct. In our new life, our greatest enemy would be laxity. It would be all too easy if, after taking an unnecessary precaution fifty times over, one omitted it just once, due to fatigue or boredom. In no time it would become a habit to forget about it; and disaster might easily follow.

I had watched carefully every word I had said to the Chauny group. They knew nothing about who we were or what our mission was; while Christine and Suzanne had been told only the bare essentials.

We had hardly started to unpack when the doorbell rang. Suzanne assured us that it was Christine; but this did not prevent us from drawing our pistols. It was Christine; and she was taken aback at being received at pistol point. Suzanne told her jokingly:

'They've been behaving like that ever since I met them; it must be the fashion in London.'

I introduced Ray to Christine. She was dying to know more about us. It was natural enough that she should be curious; but, above all, she wanted to be reassured that she was not dreaming it all. After the difficulties she had been through, she hardly dared to believe that we had brought relief.

Suzanne was going through her cupboards, and found that she had very little food, so we invited them to dinner if they could suggest a restaurant where tickets were not necessary. They knew of one and we had a good hearty meal.

On our return to the house, we were soon in a conversation about our work and our future. Ray ventured no information; he was letting me take the lead.

Christine told us what had been going on before:

'We were asked by a Frenchman, whom we have known for a long time, whether we would help in getting airmen out through Spain. We accepted, and soon we were lodging them in Paris and then sending them south.'

'Did he have any money to speak of?'

'No, he was always trying to find fresh supplies.'

'Then he had no radio contact with London?'

'He sent messages to London, but I think it was through another man. He was always expecting money but it never came. He was arrested two months ago, and since then I've been trying to carry on by borrowing.'

I gave her the 50,000 francs that I had promised her, and I

gave Suzanne 10,000 to be going on with. Money, I told them once again, was no problem.

From what Christine had said, it was plain to me that they had no idea about security. Some arrests had already taken place, and there would be more. I explained as gently as I could that we would need a new set-up, on safer lines. I would tell them what to do as we went along, and especially how to set about it; we would organize our own escape route, without anybody else knowing about it.

Christine was dubious. She asked me:

'Yes, Armand, but how will we get them out of the country?'

'We have plenty of ways lined up.'

'What will be our work then?'

'You and your friends will gather all the airmen you can and look after them in Paris. Later on you will be told where to take them. We will also set up a mobile group that will pick up airmen in the north of France.'

'You seem to want to set up a very big network.'

'Not necessarily big, but effective.'

'You will need a communication link with London.'

'That's all looked after. I hope we shall evacuate our first shipment within three or four weeks.'

'This can't be real!' she burst out. 'Why didn't you come before?' This time she was really sobbing. She must have been very desperate to feel such a relief.

She was very worried about the radio situation, and all the time she could have reached out and touched Ray's wireless case. It was tempting to open it and say, 'Here it is, take a look.' But she did not need to know, and we might just as well get used to closing off our minds to useless talk.

The discussion went on into the night. Among much else, we learnt that Suzanne's husband was a prisoner-of-war, and Christine's was a forced worker; both were in Germany. Finally we went to bed. We were tired out, for it had been a long, long day.

CHAPTER FIVE

Contact – and a Scare

1

NEXT morning we were up early to see the girls off to work. I warned them not to say a word to anyone about our arrival, and to do nothing about evacuations until we met next day. Christine said:

'But I've already arranged to put some parcels on the train at the Gare St-Lazare.'

'OK, go ahead. But they must be the last.'

When they had gone, Ray and I congratulated ourselves on our good luck so far; but we were aghast at the lack of security, or even simple common sense, in their attempts at establishing a network.

Ray then started to set up his radio in order to inform London of our safe arrival in Paris, and I put my message into cipher, not forgetting the intentional mistake, so that I would be identified. Every operator has his personal touch, so Ray would be recognized by his key work. The message had to be the correct length. If it were too long there was a risk of its being picked up by the Germans, who were listening on the air night and day; if it were too short, it would be easier for the enemy to decipher it, if they had picked it up during the transmission. A message was seldom picked up in its entirety, and this made it virtually indecipherable; but the operator would be tagged with a descriptive name, such as 'Short S', which meant that he was cutting short his S's.

The dangers inherent in the work could be minimized by

various precautions. For example, Ray never transmitted at the same hour, or from the same place, or on the same wavelength. This had all been arranged beforehand in London, so that they would know when and on what wavelength to listen out for him.

If London queried our identity, we had to insert a further deliberate mistake. But if they were sure that the cipherer or his code and key had fallen into enemy hands, they would not stop the liaison, but keep it going, first sending out true information, which the enemy could check on, and then slipping in some false information which they could not check. Because of the risk of our messages being picked up by the enemy and deciphered, they had to be kept to a minimum.

Reception, of course, was safer than transmission. In the former, the operator had only to answer the call sign by identifying himself, and then listen to the message; but during transmission he was always liable to be picked up by enemy listening stations, who promptly passed the information on to radio-detector cars. These had a system of triangulation by which they could pinpoint the location of the transmitter.

It was understandable, therefore, that an operator disliked long messages, and that as soon as he had finished sending, he wanted to return his set to its hiding place and get away from that particular spot—fast.

Everything was ready on time. I kept watch from the windows but there was no untoward activity. At the precise minute due, Ray sent out his call letters. He listened intently and you could have heard a fly in the room. No response. Again he sent out his call letters. Time stood still and so did I, listening with Ray. No answer came. What had gone wrong? Every few minutes Ray called until the half-hour allowed us went by; but there was no answer.

Ray carefully put away his set, and we held a post-mortem. I asked Ray:

'What do you think went wrong?'
'I don't know. The set's OK. I've checked everything.'
'Could it be because we're too far away?' Ray shrugged.
'The set should be powerful enough for this distance.'
'Could it be we're in a silent zone?'

'Possibly; but there's no way of finding out.'

'We'd better change sector for the next transmission, and at the same time we might just as well get a bit closer to England. How about Normandy?'

'We must try and make contact,' Ray said, 'or we're wasting our time.'

We agreed to make tracks for Normandy in time for the next rendezvous, three days later.

2

The next day was Sunday. Christine and Suzanne were not coming back to Rueil as they had to be up early to go to St-Lazare station and get their evacuees on the train to the Spanish border. They would join us in the afternoon or early evening, when we would draw up a plan for our network.

So Ray and I went out to the restaurant for a quiet lunch. Afterwards we walked at a leisurely pace back to the house. We felt well-fed and relaxed. I opened the flat door; there was a note on the floor:

'Christine and Suzanne have been *arrested*, you had better get out fast. A friend.'

We were stunned by the news. Then my brain started to work at top speed.

Presumably there were no enemy in the house or they would have picked up the note; but they might arrive at any moment. This was one occasion for fighting our way out if there were any Germans watching the house. We both went into the bedroom and got our guns.

Then I went to a front window and Ray to a rear one. Everything seemed normal; nothing moved in the deserted street. There was no question of leaving our stuff behind, we needed it too badly and there was a good chance of the Germans picking it up; besides, any trace of us in Suzanne's house would make it worse for the girls.

While Ray packed, I kept watch. Then we switched jobs. My mind was groping for an explanation. Who had brought the note? Certainly not an enemy; they would have captured us already and would certainly not have warned us. It must have been a friend; but only Christine and Suzanne knew of our existence. Had they told one of their friends about us, despite our warnings? Whoever it was must have seen them arrested, to be here so soon.

Christine and Suzanne would probably not talk, and if they did, it would not be this fast. However it was a firm rule that we should consider the Gestapo informed of what the girls knew. We completed our packing and prepared to leave. The owner's wife saw us, and said:

'A man was here asking for you.'

'We were expecting him, but not so early. He left a message for us to meet him in Paris, but unfortunately we don't know him. Can you describe him?'

She told us what he looked like in considerable detail, and said he had seemed to be in a tearing hurry. I thought we knew why even if she did not.

It sounded as if whoever it was was definitely a friend of the girls, and probably one of the team. If we could find him it would be a great help, but we didn't have a clue where to start looking.

Nobody was watching as we left the house. We left a good part of our baggage at the restaurant where we had been eating, after checking with the owner that he didn't know Suzanne, and therefore couldn't connect us with her.

I knew nobody in Paris and there was no question of going to a hotel, as the police regularly investigated the identity papers of the guests. As Ray had lived in Paris previously I asked him if he had any idea where we could go. He suggested we meet Paul Campinchi.

I had heard that name before, but where and how? Then it came back. I remembered that he had been one of the main helpers of Ray's former chief, and while a lot of others had been arrested, he had got away. This was enough to make him suspect in London, and his name had been on their list of 'doubtfuls'. Had he been lucky, or had he betrayed the others?

I told Ray what London had said about his friend, but he was quite definite. London was wrong; he would trust Campinchi. Well, it was his life as well as mine, and I thought I could trust

Ray's judgement. So I decided to talk to Campinchi and try to judge him for myself. I waited in a café while Ray went to fetch him.

They were back in twenty minutes, and I saw a middle-aged man with brown hair and a moustache, of good height and heavy-set. Later I was to find out that he was a Corsican. Something was wrong with his eyesight; he looked at me with only one eye though the other remained open. He had another very definite trait; when he was seated, he would cross his right leg over his left and shake his right foot as if he had the palsy.

I introduced myself as André, and asked him one or two questions. He just looked at me without answering. Ray said:

'I know André very well and you can trust him. We have come out from Source (London) together, and you can be as sure of him as of myself.'

Campinchi must have noticed that I had the same accent as Ray, and decided to talk. He told us how, by sheer good luck, he had missed being arrested, and had spent the past six months in hiding with his wife and daughter. When he had finished his story, I asked him whether he would consider taking up his previous work again.

'You're asking a lot,' he said. 'It's been no fun hiding out like this. My chief was a nice fellow but he would talk about his mission to anybody and everybody. The only thing he didn't do was put an ad in the papers, asking for agents for British Intelligence work.' Ray said:

'Things will be different this time. André will see to that.'

Paul was still unconvinced; but the upshot of it was that the same friend who had been hiding him and his family agreed over the phone to put us up too.

This friend was called Guette, and was quite a character. Though well over fifty, she had the looks and the vivacity of a much younger woman. She was of medium height and slim, but it was her face that held your attention: bony, and by no means beautiful, it was still tremendously alive. When she was angry or excited, her dark eyes would flash, and she was given to tossing back her long, curly and vividly hennaed hair.

She was from Algeria, and French, according to her, but I would guess that she came from the tribe of Ouled Naïl, of which I was to hear much from her later on. She was given to histrionics, and nothing was ever an ordinary, common event; it was either sublime or tragic. I put her down as the kind of person who, if she liked you, would do anything in the world for you.

The next day Ray and I went back to Rueil to get our luggage and the pistol that Ray had left under a pillow. Everything was quiet, and the owner's wife, whom we met on the doorstep, told us that the young man had not been back. Apparently the Germans had not come to search the house either, which could only mean that they had not found Suzanne's address.

So we went cautiously upstairs. There was no note under the door, nor any sign of anyone having been in the flat. We picked up the gun, took a quick look round, and got out quickly. At least if the Gestapo came now, things would not be made worse for the girls, because of us.

CHAPTER SIX

The Network Takes Shape

1

TRAVELLING in France at this time was no easy matter. Trains were few, and those that ran were well patronized by German troops, since they were less likely to be strafed by Allied aircraft than military trains. Most of the civilian passengers had been out foraging for food, and the number of pigs, chickens and pounds of butter that were carried back and forth was astonishing.

Later, like everybody else, we carried a similar freight, since to travel empty-handed would have looked thoroughly unnatural.

We were on our way to see Madame Francine Bellenger at Bourgtheroulde-Thuit-Hébert. She had been one of those who had helped me when I had escaped from the Germans after the Dieppe raid. Unfortunately, when we finally got there—after a whole night on the train—she had some visitors whom she did not trust. She said:

'The hotel keeper is a friend of mine; go to him. Tell him I sent you.'

Ray said he could perfectly well broadcast from a hotel room without anybody knowing about it; and there was no reason to mention Madame Bellenger's name, unless the proprietor refused to let us have a room, which was unlikely. In the event, he gave us an upstairs room which suited us admirably, for from it we could see far and wide over the countryside, including a good distance along the road in both directions. There were no

Germans stationed there, and so there was little danger of our being disturbed.

As before, Ray ran his aerial wire round the room. He was ready in good time; and I stood by at the window, watching for any activity or strange arrivals. It was one of those lazy sunny afternoons, with the flies buzzing the world to inactivity. We felt anything but relaxed, and hoped desperately that, this time, things would turn in our favour.

Right on the dot, Ray started sending out his call letters. I was standing close beside him, looking over his shoulder. I knew this would annoy him, and he told me so—twenty years later! However at the time I could not help myself. I was as tensed-up as he was himself.

The second call was going out now . . . and here it came, that beautiful sound of London answering Ray's call letters in morse! They had not forgotten that we existed after all! I could have yelled with delight, but did a skip instead until Ray told me to cut it out.

He fiddled with his set, then started sending his message. He listened to the repeat, corrected a passage, and signed off.

We had done it. We were in contact with Source. Ray and I shook hands and congratulated one another. In a few minutes London would know of our safe arrival, of the arrest of Christine and Suzanne and of our meeting with Campinchi. I had to tell them of this meeting, no matter how foolish it might look to them. If things went wrong, they would know where to look for culprits. In fact the subject was never mentioned, then or later.

2

The return to Paris was a nightmare. The first train we took was crowded, the second was overcrowded and the third was so overfull that try as we might, we could not get on, and were left on the platform. As the train was pulling out, a civilian opened a door and jumped off. As that door came up to us, we ran with the train and jumped in—right into the coach reserved for the *Wehrmacht*!

It was the German police who had thrown off the civilian; but for some reason they had immediately gone back into the coach, and some German soldiers standing in the corridor just smiled. Most troops do not particularly like their own military police and will not necessarily help them against civilians. This seemed to be the case here.

They could also have been smiling, of course, because they knew we would be thrown off as soon as the police found us. They did come back a few minutes later, and went mad when they saw us. They had got rid of one civilian and found two instead. They asked the soldiers why they had not closed the door. Nobody answered. The train was now travelling fast, sixty or seventy miles an hour; if they tried to throw us off we should have to fight.

The NCO in charge took a look outside the door and closed it. We let out our breath. Then he yelled at us again, demanded our papers, examined them briefly, and told us we must get off at the next stop.

When at last we were left alone, a soldier who spoke fair French told us not to worry, the next stop was Villeneuve-St-Georges and from there we could go into Paris by bus. He went on to tell us about himself. He had no love for the army, and was taking some food back to his family in Germany.

It felt very queer, standing there talking to an enemy soldier as if he were simply a casual acquaintance, when all the time I could feel the weight of a rifle in my hands and imagine ramming the bayonet into his belly.

When we stopped at Villeneuve-St-Georges, he told us to go back to the other end of the train and try to find a place in the civilian coach. This we did, with considerable difficulty, and had no more trouble from the MPs.

At St-Lazare station, several windows were broken as we all struggled to climb out. We were packed so tight we could not open the doors.

3

Back at Guette's place, I resumed the discussion with Paul. I found him to be an intelligent and wary man; and his wariness had been intensified by his recent experiences. It was what I was looking for—someone who would keep his mouth shut and talk only when it was absolutely necessary.

Eventually he agreed to take over control of the Paris region and its suburbs. He would choose a man who could organize a group of guides to go into the country and bring in baled-out airmen and others whose presence was required back in England. These guides would convoy them to whatever destination we selected.

In addition, Paul agreed to try and find someone to supply lodgings and food for the evacuees in and around Paris, and a printer to undertake the manufacture of false identity papers. He would also need a sort of quartermaster who would go round searching for food and clothing. We agreed to look for a suitable English-speaking person to act as interpreter and work with the lodging master.

Rules on security were laid down as follows:

1. All agents to keep their addresses secret.
2. Chiefs to meet their inferiors only when necessary, and never to give them information that was not absolutely essential.
3. Work through accommodation addresses.
4. Agents to avoid friendly meetings with one another.
5. Contacts between guides and lodgers to be carried out by pre-arranged signals.
6. Evacuees to be passed along the line without their guides meeting one another.
7. Nobody to talk about his chief, or admit to having one.
8. The head of the network to remain completely unknown.
9. Evacuees not to be told of the existence of a network.
10. All evacuees to be interrogated as soon as taken in charge.

The purpose of laying down rules was twofold: first, to impress on the members of the network the idea that they were professionals, and were not therefore at liberty to gab as they pleased; and second, to prevent the enemy from infiltrating our network with bogus airmen.

Stopping careless talk was not an easy task, especially where Frenchmen were concerned. They liked to expatiate on the fact that they were doing something for their country; and after that it only needed one of their friends to talk in front of an acquaintance who was a *collaborateur*.

Although it was necessary to shut off agents and sections from one another, it was difficult to achieve. Everyday life had to go on. But it was vital; in the event of an arrest, such ignorance could save a lot of agents' lives.

The infiltration of false airmen was a real headache. The enemy would place an English-speaking man, dressed in a captured flying suit, near a farm—usually one suspected of having helped airmen or at least of being pro-British—and he would ask for help. He would be passed along from one hide-out to another; and when he had gone as far as possible he would come out and report to the nearest German post. In this way a whole network could be busted.

It was possible to prevent this happening by insisting on the confirmation of the identity of any evacuee taken in charge. This was not difficult; most of the airmen came in batches, from one plane; they knew each other well, and they tried hard to stick together.

The fighter pilot, on the other hand, was usually alone, and he was top priority, especially if he were from the RAF. But he could nearly always be identified by his accent, and his knowledge of England and of recent events there, such as shows, films and race meetings. With British airmen we could check on their knowledge of cricket, while with Americans it was baseball.

4

Campinchi was soon carrying out the plans we had discussed, recruiting personnel among his friends and acquaintances, on the assurance that they would be working for the Allied cause—they were willing to work for France, but not for Vichy—that security would be strict, and that money was available.

In the meantime Ray and I were discovering sources of food in the black market. Prices were high, but as soon as it was learnt that we could pay, the sources multiplied. We avoided being seen too much by the neighbours, and went out mostly at night. We went only to the local cinema, as the downtown ones were often raided, especially in daytime.

Our next step was to find a way out of France. Following Pat O'Leary's example, I decided that we would try Brittany. First of all, we needed a contact, and here we were lucky. Ray remembered having met a Dr Le Balch from the Côtes du Nord when he had been studying in Paris, and set about finding him.

He was successful; and it turned out that the doctor had recently completed his qualifications and had bought a practice in Plouézec, some twenty miles from Plouha. We arranged to visit him as soon as he had moved, which would be in a week or two.

Campinchi had already picked up some parcels and was getting them together in Paris, but as we still had no way out of France this was rather jumping the gun. They would have been better off in the country where food was cheaper and more plentiful; but Campinchi wanted to get his organization running in good time, and I accepted his argument.

In the meantime, the fact that Campinchi, Ray and I were all living in the same apartment was a risk; if one got into trouble the other two were bound to be involved; so we arranged to separate. We found a place to store all the dangerous equipment we had with us, including our money. A friend gave us permission to use a maid's room in the 18th Arrondissement, not far from Guette's place. It was already used as a storeroom and a little more would be neither here nor there. We told her that our cases which were strong and well locked, contained clothes we did not need.

As soon as we had the key, we went to a locksmith and had a duplicate made. This would allow us free access, without our friend's knowing about it, the only problem being the *concierge*, as we had no apparent business in the building. One might say it was hardly the way to treat a friend, but we were not concerned about that. She was an elderly woman, and the less she knew about what we were up to the better for her. For this reason, we never told her where we were staying. We had found a safe hiding place for our guns and ammunition, the plans of operations, simplified codes, microfilms, radio equipment and money. We did not like leaving the last there, in case of theft, but there was no other solution. Banks were out of the question, and we could not entrust it to anyone else. We kept a good reserve with us at all times.

At least I knew then that I was 'clean': there was nothing on or about me that could give me away, except the contact with Campinchi, and I was trying to sever this. Ray had kept his radio set, as he needed it often, but he found another cache for it and did not tell me where it was. I could not use the set, as I was no radio operator, so it was better for me to know nothing about it. Communications were his domain.

Guette had a friend who managed a hotel close by, and I took a room there. This was not the best solution, as she, as well as Campinchi, his wife Thérèse and Ray would all know where I lived, but it was an improvement on all of us living together.

At the same time Ray rented a room from some friends. He did not give his new address to Guette or Campinchi, and he and I would meet only for essential business.

It was at Guette's house that I met a friend of hers, Marcelle. She was beautiful, had a good figure, and was studying in Paris to be a singer. When I told her I was a stranger in the city, she offered to take me round. We dined often together, went to several shows, and life became much pleasanter. I told her that I was a French officer who had escaped from Germany, and that I did not dare to return to my home in Morvan for fear of being recognized. This story, which I also whispered to the hotel manager, would allay suspicions, and also attract sympathy from my French *compatriotes*, Gaullist and Vichyist alike.

I had most of my meals in the hotel room. The cuisine was excellent, and the chef was famous for his *Soufflé au fromage*. When one of these was brought into the dining room, as high as the chef's white cap and with a smell to make one's mouth water, there would be a moment of silence and admiration, not only for the beauty of it, but also for the adroitness of the cook in managing to muster the ingredients in those days of austerity.

One day I was told by Guette that Marcelle had failed her exam at the *Comédie Française*, and needed consoling. We had been seeing a lot of one another; and I had an idea that any personal charm on my part was not the sole attraction, but that Guette, who was very money-conscious, had slipped in a word that I kept a well-stacked wallet. This was an opportunity to put the matter to the test. I invited her to dinner at my hotel.

After a good meal and an excellent bottle of wine, she felt much better, and so did I. The renowned soufflé appeared; and then I ordered coffee and liqueurs to be served in my room. I had been a reluctant bachelor for some time, and it wasn't long before I discovered that our thoughts were running along similar lines.

She had a birth-mark just below her lip; and I soon learnt that she also had a dark spot under the nipple of her left breast. The monastic orders we had been given in England were forgotten, and she only just caught the last *métro* home.

CHAPTER SEVEN

Preparing the Ground

1

PLOUÉZEC, where Dr Le Balch was taking up his practice, was in a restricted zone. Many of the residents had been compelled to move out, and in order to visit the area it was necessary to procure a temporary permit from the German authorities. We had no intention of revealing anything about ourselves to the enemy, and so I asked Campinchi to organize an *Ausweiss* for Ray and myself.

His printer made a good job of them, and armed with these, we were able to make reservations on the train to St Brieuc. This was a new regulation, one of a whole set introduced by the Germans as the tide of war turned against them, all of them calculated to make a job like ours more exacting.

Before we left Paris, I sent out strict verbal instructions on security to the members of the network; I did not want any relaxation of precautions while we were away.

The journey, which was considerably more comfortable than previous ones, passed off without incident. Our permits withstood the scrutiny of the gendarmes and the German police at St Brieuc. The luggage that contained the wireless, which had been our main worry, was fortunately not examined.

From St Brieuc we caught *le petit train départemental* for Plouézec. This train was a real museum piece, so enfeebled by age and, I dare say, poor coal, that at each incline the passengers had to get out and push. On the flat it achieved a shattering 15 mph.

Eventually we got to Plouézec and found the doctor waiting for us. His family were still in Paris so he had his spacious house to himself, which simplified the problem of lodging for us, as we were not particularly fond of hotels. He told his maid, Marie, that we were both doctors, visiting him on business; I was a regular doctor but no longer practising, while Ray was a medical student, selling remedial electrical apparatus. This checked with his papers and explained his electrical case.

2

The next day Ray had a rendezvous with London. He set up the radio in his room, while I went downstairs to head off Marie and keep watch. Finally Ray made contact. My previous message was acknowledged, and I was again warned against Campinchi. More disturbing was the news that the Gestapo were very active, and most of the British agents had been arrested. We were some of the last left in the field.

The first contact Le Balch organized for us was Henri Le Blais, wheat controller for the department. I had a chat with him, and decided to tell him about our project for operation 'Bonaparte'—a plan for shipping out escaped airmen by sea— and he was very willing to work with us. He was deeply impressed at meeting a member of the British Intelligence Service, and he could be a valuable ally, for he knew everybody, travelled a lot, and last but not least, was allowed to drive a car.

As we parted that night, I recommended the utmost secrecy and discretion, and insisted that he was not to tell anybody about our meeting. However, I quickly discovered that, after leaving me, he had gone straight to his brother, who lived a few doors away, and told him and his wife all he knew.

I was furious, and told him so. He protested that his brother, who was the Secrétaire de Mairie, and his sister-in-law were completely trustworthy. So they might be: what I did not like was that he had had to tell somebody. It suggested to me immediately that he was a blabber, and I gave him a piece of my mind.

In spite of this bad start he drove us round looking for a

likely spot for embarkation and likely people to help us, and I was glad to see he did not tell anybody who I was or what we were up to. He was allowed a small quantity of petrol by the German authorities, and they checked his milometer at regular intervals. He equally regularly disconnected it. He kept the petrol for starting in the morning, after that he would switch to alcohol, which he could buy freely from the farmers, who distilled it themselves. He kept the main tank full of alcohol, and had a second tank fitted under the bonnet for petrol. He could switch over from one to the other at will.

On our trips, Le Blais introduced us to a number of Bretons. Their hospitality was heart-warming; in fact, their one ambition on meeting strangers seemed to be to see how fast they could get them drunk. They considered it an insult if one left their house without eating and drinking.

On one of these visits, I found myself faced with an unexpected hazard of my new occupation. We were eating sardines cooked on the hearth, accompanied by home-made bread, and the usual potations, when I was told that the farmer's wife at a neighbouring farm was expecting a baby that evening, and that her pains had already started. Le Blais, of course, had introduced me as a doctor, so everyone felt that there was nothing to worry about.

The only one who was worrying was myself. I asked, very casually, if Dr Le Balch had been warned, to be told that somebody had gone off on a bicycle to fetch him but that he was out on a call. They had left a message for him to come at once.

Time passed, and there was no sign of the doctor. The calls from the neighbouring farm became more and more pressing, and finally I decided that I should have to go and put up a show. I was well aware that the women present probably knew far more about childbirth than I did, but I reckoned I could get away with pretending to supervise the event while actually keeping well out of it. I could always say that I did not want to spoil my clothes.

I was attempting to put this rather feeble plan into operation when a motor-assisted bicycle drew up outside. It was Le Balch, and I breathed a sigh of relief; but the doctor had to have his little joke. Instead of taking care of everything and forgetting about me, he insisted that he needed help, and as a doctor and his guest, I could not refuse him. I was quite used to seeing people die, but it was the first time that I had seen one born, and I do not mind admitting I did not feel too good!

Le Balch played the same trick on me on another occasion when we picked up a woman who had come off her bicycle and cut her head badly. We took her back to the surgery, and again the doctor was out. Again, arriving in the nick of time, he roped me in to help him. I was obviously in danger of becoming indispensable, though I suppose my presence lent credibility to the role in which he had cast me.

3

Le Blais introduced me to François Le Cornec, a friend of his, who ran a café and charcuterie in Plouha, and who was the head of the local Resistance. He was just the man I was looking for to take charge of the beach during 'Bonaparte', and we went together to inspect the spot we had agreed in London.

It was about five miles north of Plouha, and the beach itself —shingle, and then sand that would be uncovered for fifty yards at low tide—was fine. The only snag was that behind it was a sheer cliff, a hundred feet high.

A hundred yards to the south was a small cove with a road leading to a quay, but in front of it there were a lot of submerged rocks. Maybe this was the place that London had meant for 'Bonaparte'; in which case they could not have known about the rocks. Small boats coming in there at night would be wrecked in any sort of sea, and it was obvious that the rocks had been put there with exactly that idea in mind.

At low tide we could reach the beach from the quay and make our way round to the next cove, but at high tide it would be impossible. We went back to the cliff and found that by taking it at an angle it could be descended; it meant more or less sliding down on our backsides, but as the people we visualized using it would be young, fit and only too anxious to get away, this was not a serious objection.

I asked Le Cornec whether he were willing to act as beach

master, and he agreed, so we went on to discuss details. The escapers would arrive at St Brieuc, where Le Blais would take charge of them. From there, Le Cornec's group would escort them in the departmental train, and hide them in farmhouses around Plouha. Le Cornec himself would supply all the guides and arrange the lodgings, as well as providing a special group to look after the operation proper.

I found Le Cornec to be a wary and discreet man. He thought out a problem and did not speak until he had reached a reasoned solution. Everything was falling into place nicely, and I felt the time had come to trigger off the first operation.

I sent a message to London, telling them that all the arrangements for 'Bonaparte' were complete, and asking them to send weapons, various items we needed, more money and a more powerful radio set. We did not intend to use it unless really forced to, as we had no desire to be picked up by every receiver in France and Germany; but it seemed a wise precaution to have it, since without communications we could do nothing.

With that done, and the network I had built up committed to its first testing, I gave Le Blais a final briefing, enough money to keep him going, and an address and the procedure by which to find me in Paris, and left him to it. He would be the only person who knew how to get in touch with me.

CHAPTER EIGHT

Operation Bonaparte

1

CAMPINCHI had enough parcels ready to make the operation worth while. The first moonless night was 15 December, and I sent a message to London asking them to lay on 'Bonaparte' then. The acceptance came in that evening, and I told Campinchi when to get his men moving to St Brieuc. Then away I went, by myself this time, to Brittany to tie up the final arrangements with Le Blais and Le Cornec.

There were fifteen parcels, and their despatching went without a hitch. They were taken to Montparnasse station, and handed over to their new guides, who put them on the train. Their instructions being that they were exhausted workers, they had all immediately fallen into a deep sleep. Towards the end of the journey, the guides slipped them their new identity papers and an *Ausweiss* prepared by the Paris printer.

At St Brieuc, they passed through the gate just like all the other passengers. They were taken to a nearby café where the Plouha guides took over, again on recognition signals. They were then moved to Plouha, a few at a time and mostly at night; otherwise the number of strangers appearing in a small town might have aroused suspicion.

Ray joined me in St Brieuc. He had his wireless set, though we did not expect to need it, and in any case it was dangerous to broadcast from Plouha. I hated his travelling with it; he was always in danger of being searched at the barrier by the French police, acting on the orders of their German masters. Ideally he should have one wherever it might be needed, and I made a mental note to ask for several extra sets.

Driven by Henri Le Blais, and under Le Cornec's orders, we moved into his place, unseen and unheard. I may have been Monsieur Léon (my name in Brittany), the big boss, but to Le Cornec I was just another risk. He was taking no chances, and for this I admired him very much.

A small dining room connected the café with his living quarters. He locked the door leading into the café, and as long as we did not make too much noise we could remain there undetected. Above, we had a room with two beds.

That evening we celebrated the coming operation. The weather was bad, with a gale blowing. It was bitterly cold, but the heavy dinner and the drinks kept us comfortable.

Next morning we woke late, but even so the day dragged. It was still cold and blowing. Every now and then we would do physical jerks, just to keep the blood circulating. There was nothing to do but sit and talk, and sometimes take a look at the weather vane on top of the church next door, being careful that nobody should see us at the window.

At six o'clock we switched on Le Cornec's old radio, and listened to the BBC programme *Les français parlent aux français*. This was strictly forbidden by the Germans, but most of the French population listened to it, whatever their opinions, just to get news from the outside world as a change from German propaganda. After the news came the personal messages. These were, in reality, disguised instructions to the maquis or the networks, and 'Bonaparte' had three messages prearranged for transmission on this programme.

We had to listen intently, because the Germans were deliberately trying to mask it by interference. Towards the end, there was a message for us: '*Yvonne pense souvent à l'heureuse occasion*.' We were disappointed, but did not immediately show it as we had not told Le Cornec about the system. He switched off the set, and I said:

'Because of the gale, the operation is postponed for twenty-four hours.'

Disgusted, we went off to our beds only to find that they were full of fleas. Every now and again we would get up and brush them out, and then of course we started shivering again.

We spent nine miserable days in those rooms, freezing in the daytime, freezing at night, and chasing fleas. How we would have welcomed some good flea powder!

On the ninth day we got a message finally putting off the operation. It hardly came as a surprise, for the gale had been blowing all the time, but it was a severe disappointment nevertheless. I arranged with Le Cornec and Francis Baudet, his assistant, to leave the parcels in Brittany until the next attempt, on 28 January. They would be less trouble in the country, and Le Cornec arranged to move them out of the town into farmhouses where they could play mute farm labourers or aliens. It would be safer than holding them in the town itself. As for Ray and me, there was nothing further we could do in Brittany, so we returned to Paris, with the prospect of a month's vacation in front of us.

2

Campinchi reported that more and more airmen were coming into Paris as we established new contacts, and it was imperative that we extend the network and try to find another escape route, if possible not by sea. Aeroplanes were useless for our purposes, as bombers could not land in the small fields available, and light planes could only take out two men at a time, which was adequate for agents, but not for parties like ours. There remained the southern border, and the passes through the Pyrenees.

The route had certain disadvantages. It meant several days of marching through the mountains, which might be too much for those who were in poor condition or badly shod; and for those who did succeed in crossing the border into Spain there was a good chance of being picked up by the Spanish police and left to rot in prison camps. This was hardly the object of the exercise.

Nevertheless, I thought it worth putting out some feelers. The guides were mostly ex-peacetime smugglers who had trafficked in cigarettes or any other merchandise that would bring a profit, and there were reports that some of them had taken evacuees up into the mountains and lost some or all of them, only to come back and claim payment. I thought I had a way of getting that straightened out when necessary.

In the meantime I had other things on my mind. In the first place, it was time I moved from the hotel, where I could be traced via Le Balch and Campinchi, and I set about looking for a flat. They were hard to find, but the fact that I was able to pay top prices helped, and after a time I was offered exactly what I wanted in the Avenue Charles Floquet, just off the Champ-de-Mars. It belonged to a journalist who had been assigned to Switzerland; it was on the sixth floor, overlooking half Paris, and it was fully furnished even down to linen and tableware. I moved in, making sure I wasn't followed; the only person to whom I gave the address was Ray, and he was instructed only to come there in the direst emergency. If he phoned, it must be only from a public call-box.

Now, with a reasonably secure headquarters, Ray and I were able to clear our things out of the maid's room where we had cached them. We were living apart and saw as little of each other as possible. The less one link in the chain was seen to be connected with another, the safer we were. I kept the key to the maid's room, however, and established a hide-out there with spare clothes, food and a new set of papers. If I ever did have to disappear, I could hole up there for weeks and emerge as a completely different character.

A problem of a rather awkward kind concerned the fair Marcelle. She had begun pressing me to buy more and more clothes and things, not for herself, she said, but for Guette, who had introduced us, and in the end I became wary and decided to find out what she was up to. A young civil servant I knew by the name of Jean Mettling, who had done some work with the Resistance and knew a bit about police investigations, agreed to look into her private life for me. I had an ulterior motive in this, because I needed someone like him to form a security section; if he succeeded with Marcelle, it would give me a good idea of his capabilities; if he failed, nothing would be lost.

It did not take Jean long to discover that she was working the streets as a common prostitute. Guette had introduced her to me as a personal friend; had she told Marcelle who I was? There was one way to find out, and that was to invite her to come and live with me. If she agreed, it would mean she regarded me simply as a mystery man with plenty of money; if she refused, I could be pretty certain she knew what I was up to. I put the question to her one evening in the hotel, not long before I was due to move, and her reaction was instantaneous and definite: no. That settled it. I didn't see her again, and I made sure she didn't know where I had moved to. Nor did I give my new address to Guette.

So the month slipped quickly past, and it was time, once again, to try and launch 'Bonaparte' on the stormy waters of the English Channel.

3

Ray and I travelled to Brittany in good time. We brought along a supply of flea powder, and it was not so cold. The day before the operation, Le Cornec collected the parcels from the farms where they had been staying and brought them into Plouha.

The weather was fair, but we tried to keep our hopes down, just in case. At six o'clock, in company with Le Cornec, we tuned into the BBC in the small room next to the café. The third message came: *'Bonjour, tout le monde à la maison d'Alphonse.'* That was what we had been waiting for. It was for us, and it meant that the operation was on for that night. We could have yelled for joy, but instead we kept straight faces and listened to the end of the bulletin, not only because the café was full of people, but also because it was better if Le Cornec did not know which message was ours. When I looked up with a great big smile on my face, he did not have to be told the good news to bring out a bottle. Our toast was: 'To success and a busy season.'

Le Cornec and I went through our plan again. We had to wait for confirmation on the nine o'clock news. If all was well, two of our helpers would go and tell the runners to warn the guides to start moving the parcels, each by a separate route, to the rendezvous at Jean Gicquel's house, known later as *La Maison d'Alphonse*. They were to be there at eleven thirty.

In the meantime, we had supper, although we were so excited we could hardly sit down. At nine o'clock the confirmation came; it meant that the boat had left her English port and had not turned back. I said:

'Let's go.'

Everybody departed, except Ray. He looked very dejected at being left behind, but we might not come back, and somebody would have to report the fact to Source. A curfew was in force and German patrols were about; we had a very good chance of being shot or falling into an ambush. My equipment consisted of a heavy pistol, plenty of ammunition, two flashlights, a piece of cardboard, two rubber bands, a blue transparent plastic disc, a bottle of cognac, some wrapping paper and string.

Le Cornec had a pistol of his own, and Ray had loaned his two, and I my small one, so all the men on the escort would be armed. We were ready to fight it out with the enemy if it became necessary.

Le Cornec and I travelled together, avoiding the main street, and using footpaths as soon as we were in the open. We could follow the progress of our different groups by the barking of the farm dogs. Everyone came in at the rendezvous in good time, with Le Cornec checking the furtive entry of each lot and Francis Baudet, his assistant, sorting them out. The parcels were put in the farthest room, and the operators in the kitchen-bedroom.

Although each man knew his job backwards, Le Cornec went through a dress rehearsal with the operators. They were, besides Le Cornec and Baudet, Pierre Huet (called Tarzan) chief guide, Job Mainguy assistant guide and in charge of light signals (he had been in the navy), Marie-Thérèse Le Calvez, Le Cornec's liaison agent, Jean Trihiou a local farmer, and Jean Gicquel, who would cover the rear and make sure that we were not being followed.

When Le Cornec had done, it was my turn to brief the airmen, who for a month had been living by twos and threes, mostly in farmhouses, without a clue as to what would happen next. Now all seventeen had been brought together to this room on the coast; little wonder if they were bewildered.

Up to this point I had been just another Frenchman to them. Now, quite unexpectedly, I spoke English, without a French accent.

'Well, fellows, this is the last lap of a long journey. It is the last, but the most dangerous one. We are about a mile from the Channel; if everything goes well, you'll be aboard a British warship in two hours and in England by nine o'clock in the morning.'

There were excited but subdued sounds of joy. I went on:

'When the guides get ready to leave, you will form up in single file. The first man will hold on to the coat tail of the third guide, Marie-Thérèse. Each one will hold on to the coat tail of the man in front. There's no moon, and if you don't hang on you'll lose sight of the man you are following. If you do lose him, stand still and make no noise; the guides will straighten you out.

'When you reach the coast, you'll have to go down a steep cliff. Lie on your backs and slide down. When you get to the bottom you'll be told where to sit.

'There will be no smoking, talking, or coughing, either on the way or on the beach. Small boats will come in to pick you up. When ordered to, and not before, you will wade out to the boats and get in.

'Here is a package for the senior officer. Who is he?'

'Here.'

'When you get to England give this bottle of cognac to the first British security officer who meets you at the docks. You're responsible for seeing that it reaches England. If you're attacked, destroy it: ashore, break it on a rock and throw it in the bushes; at sea, drop it overboard, it'll sink.'

'That must be a valuable bottle of cognac.'

'It is. Who's next in rank?'

'I am.' I handed him a small folded piece of paper.

'Keep this in your hand till you get on board. If we're attacked, put it in your mouth, chew it thoroughly and swallow it. Otherwise it must be delivered with the bottle of cognac.

'If we're attacked, you are all expected to fight. Some of the guides have pistols, but if you have a knife, use it. If not, use your hands, your feet or your teeth. If you get your hands on somebody, make sure it's a German, and then show what you can do.

'If you get lost, any farmer in the vicinity will help you, and you only risk going to a POW camp, so don't say anything about this set-up. Your guide is risking his life and that of his family, so give him a chance. Any questions?'

'Yes, who are *you*?'

Several others asked me the same thing. Who was I? Who, indeed? I said:

'Never mind; and if anybody asks you, just tell them you were talking to Captain Harrison. That's all, so—good-bye and good luck!'

London did not know me under the name of Captain Harrison but they would soon guess who it was from the description. I had invented it on the spur of the moment; name-changing had become automatic.

The very valuable bottle of cognac was just that, and Colonel Langley would appreciate it; but he would appreciate even more the thirty-page report of our activities, closely handwritten the night before and wrapped round it. To make things a bit more difficult if it fell into German hands, I had replaced all names and addresses by numbers, and the index of these numbers, with the corresponding information, was carried by the second man who had the job of chewing the bit of folded paper.

In all these precautions, I was always conscious of the possibility of getting caught. We were far past the stage of calculated risks; there were too many to calculate. It was a matter of eliminating as many as possible.

4

At midnight we told everyone to get ready. We turned out the light, opened the door, and were confronted with an inky darkness. Pierre Huet was at the head of the column. We waited for two minutes to accustom our eyes to the blackness, and then moved off towards the beach.

On one occasion the chain was broken. Le Cornec, who was in the rear, went ahead to find the break, raced forward to stop Pierre Huet, and got everybody together again. When we got to the cliff-edge, we could see the waves below us, a long, long way down. I was one of the last to slide, and although I was careful to keep leaning backwards, I could feel myself almost rolling forward head first. It was a wonder nobody was hurt.

I had given one torch to Job Mainguy, who knew morse. He stayed at the top of the cliff to signal to the incoming boats. A cardboard tube masked it, so it could be seen only from seaward. The code was the letter 'B', at one minute intervals.

I had given the other flashlight to Marie-Thérèse. She was at sea level, and kept flashing it on and off all the time. Her light had the blue plastic screen and was not visible from very far away.

To right and left of us, at 500 yards' distance, were German listening posts; but with the darkness and the noise of the sea, it was unlikely they would spot us. Ten miles away, on the Pointe de Guilben, there was a radar installation and a battery of medium guns, but they were the navy's worry, not ours.

At about a quarter past one, we saw three dark spots on the sea. We watched them intently. They were not an illusion, they were moving slowly towards the shore. I waded out to the centre one, flanked by Le Cornec and Huet, pistols drawn, ready to fire. A figure jumped off the bows and came closer. I called out the password:

'Dinan.'

'St Brieuc,' came the reply.

What a relief! It was the Royal Navy after all. I put away my pistol and waved my arms to the operators. They quickly unloaded the incoming stores, and then brought the men out and saw them into the boats. In twelve minutes they were rowing back to their parent ship, with seventeen very happy parcels with them. Both sailors and passengers would be glad to get clear of that hostile coast.

As for us, we were pleased enough to wade ashore again.

This was January in the English Channel, not summer on the Côte d'Azur. We were wet to our shoulders, and the water was so cold that, even with the excitement, it choked the breath out of us. We hauled and dragged the cases of stores up the cliff, and wasted no time in marching back to the *Maison d'Alphonse.*

5

We had some hot coffee with cognac, and although the kitchen was warm, we went on shivering for a long time.

Six cases had come in; they were all alike, all beautifully packed. I was so elated that the operation had gone off smoothly that I made a silly mistake, and opened them in front of the operators. They contained, apart from weapons, ammunition, a wireless set, chocolate, cigarettes, coffee, whisky and many other items—virtually everything I had asked for—together with four million francs. The money was all in one case, good, worn ten thousand franc notes, pressed (not ironed) into tight bundles, and I felt a stir of expectancy round me.

I gave the .45 Colts and their ammunition to Le Cornec, and distributed some of the luxuries to the operators. Then I closed the cases, remarking that the rest was for other members of the organization. I had discussed with Le Cornec how much he would give to each person, and he had paid them accordingly; but seeing all this money, they imagined I was going to dish it out by the fistful.

I could not pretend, even to myself, that they were getting paid adequately for the risks they were taking; those were beyond computation. But we did not want anybody working purely for money. We paid a good wage, plus expenses; to overpay had its own dangers. Some people lose their heads when they get a bit of money, start drinking heavily, and then start talking. In addition, if a number of people in a small town suddenly appeared flush, the word would quickly get around and suspicions might be aroused.

With Le Cornec's help, I took the money to Marie-Thérèse's house, where her mother had been waiting up for us all night.

13 The cliff down which airmen were
~~led~~ to the beach

14 The author's identity card when
he operated under the name of Lucien
Jules Desbien

15 The author at the Operation Bonaparte reunion in Buffalo; with him
(left to right) are Raymond Labrosse, the Deputy Commanding Officer in
Shelburn, Anita Lemonnier, Special Interrogator in Paris and Mathurin
Branchoux, the leader of the resistance in Guingamp

16 A plaque attached to the rocks above 'Bonaparte beach' commemorating the work of the Shelburn network and the men who lost their lives for it

We had more coffee and cognac, and I went to bed. Le Cornec would pass on the glad news to Ray on his way home.

The room was fairly warm and there were lots of blankets on the bed, but I was still woken, at noon, by cold feet. To this day I shudder at the coldness of that water.

6

Later in the afternoon Le Blais drove up in his car. The smile on his face was proof that he had heard the news. I sent him off to the *Maison d'Alphonse* to pick up the other suitcases and take them to St Brieuc. On the way he dropped me at Le Cornec's place, where we had a little celebration. Ray was delighted to have the bigger wireless set, for it meant that our radio communications were well catered for.

Le Blais had managed to arrange sleepers for us on the Paris train, and as I turned in to the rhythmic clickety-clack of the wheels, I looked back over all that had happened since my first train ride in France. I remembered whistling *Un Canadien Errant* on the railway embankment to try and find Vermette and Cloutier, after we had jumped; and, before that, the desperate battle on the beaches of Dieppe. I had been lucky to get away. Now I was back in France, under very different circumstances, and thirteen American airmen, four RAF men, and two Frenchmen, who had been part of the network with Le Cornec and were under suspicion from the Gestapo, were safely on their way to England. I felt I was on the way to repaying my debt to all who had helped me.

London had said that I could send fifteen parcels per operation, but I had increased the number to nineteen. I didn't think a few more would make any difference to the navy, but each man was one more trained flier saved to help carry on the war.

I saw no reason why the network shouldn't repeat the operation. There was always the possibility that it might come to an abrupt end; but even if Ray and I were killed, we would still be in credit on the deal. Those nineteen lives could not be taken away from us; and whatever they achieved in the future was partly due to us, just as whatever I was achieving was partly due to Pat O'Leary.

With such complacent and self-congratulatory thoughts running through my mind, I drifted off to sleep. My mood might have been very different if I had known what was awaiting me in Paris.

CHAPTER NINE

Shelburn at Risk*

1

AT Montparnasse all was well. Ray and I went our separate ways, and I took the *métro* to Lamarck-Caulincourt. As I stepped out of the station, I ran straight into a barrage of Parisian police. They were searching all bags and parcels, and I still had two, one of them full of money. It was a ticklish situation.

I had come across these snap searches before, and I knew that plain-clothes policemen mixed in the crowd and watched for people who turned back. These would be picked up for special attention, so that was out of the question. Supervising the whole thing would be German policemen in civilian clothes, and they would be there to check that the Parisian police were doing their duty.

I could try dropping the suitcase with the money, but there was always the risk that, even it it were not noticed, someone would bump into it and draw attention to it. And the two suitcases were identical.

The people without parcels were already going off to the left, while the others were bunched on the right, moving very slowly, and dividing into files to go through the search-point.

I had good papers and a good story, but they would only hold up so far; no false papers can withstand thorough investigation. In any case, honest men did not cart four million francs in cash

---

* This was the name by which our escape network was known in London.

about with them in a suitcase. There was just one chance. The police were not working in pairs, as they usually did; if I could find a young one, I might be able to scare him into letting me through. Some *gendarmes*, I knew, had been killed by the Resistance for zealousness in the service of the Germans. Better still, I might be lucky and hit on an anti-German one.

I chose my man carefully. He was young, and did not look too tough. When my turn came, I jokingly told him that my cases were full of grenades and machine-guns. He gave me a quick glance and said in a moderate tone:

'Open up.'

I stepped aside while I searched for my keys. It would give him time to think over the situation. The person behind me was passed through, and for a moment nobody else was in earshot. I whispered:

'If you look into those cases, you're a dead man. I'm not alone and the others have your number.'

Roughly he repeated his order:

'Open up.'

Obviously threats were not going to work, so I muttered:

'All right then, you're either with me or against me.'

The change was immediate. He said, almost apologetically:

'The inspectors are watching, so you'd better open them. We're searching for food.'

'It's up to you,' I said, and handed him the keys.

He lifted a handful of clothes out of my personal case, then picked up a shirt from the other one and saw the money. Casually he told me to close the cases.

'Where did you get it?'

'It's Resistance money,' I said.

'Go on. Clear out.'

I did as I was told, though I had some doubts as to whether my legs would carry me to the nearest bench. If he had so much as lifted a finger towards one of the inspectors, my goose would have been cooked. Certainly it was as close to the Gestapo as I ever wished to be.

At about this time, as it happened, the entire network was threatened. Claudette (Marie-Rose Zerling, the chief lodger and Paris interrogator) had interrogated a reputed airman by the name of Olafson and doubted whether he was genuine. He was lodging in Paris with two American airmen, who were suspicious of him because he knew nothing about flying. I decided to talk to him myself.

His story was that he was Norwegian and he had sailed to England in a small boat with his two brothers, one of whom was now living in a large town in the south west of England, and the other of whom was a sergeant in the Armoured Corps. Olafson himself had been sent to the USA, near Boston, to complete a radio course, and had then returned to England where, according to his story, he had been employed making recordings of a bomber in action over Germany for transmission by the BBC. He had been in an American plane over Hamburg when they were hit, and he had parachuted to safety. All he knew about the plane was that the pilot's name was Lieutenant Wood.

Was he genuine or not? If not, and we let him remain in the network, some 200 people might land in the hands of the Gestapo. We could not afford to make a mistake.

He spoke indifferent English with a strong Scandinavian accent. I questioned him closely for forty-five minutes, and I was far from satisfied; but I did not want him to run out on us at this stage. So I hedged; but before I left, I took one of the Americans aside, gave him my gun and told him to watch Olafson day and night. If he made any attempt to get away he was to shoot him dead.

What Olafson did not know was that we could check much of his story very quickly. A short emergency radio message was all that was required. Forty-eight hours later came the answer: 'No trace of Olafson with the Americans. No trace of his brother at the address given. No record of his brother with the Armoured Corps.'

For good measure, since a man's life might be at stake, I

asked them to check again. The answer was curt: 'Definitely no such man. Get rid of him quickly.'

In the meantime Olafson had succeeded in giving the Americans the slip and had vanished. Through Jean Mettling, whom I had put on the case, we later discovered that he was Danish and working for the Gestapo. From the crude way in which he had been planted, I came to the conclusion that it was a routine operation, and that the network itself was still not compromised, but it showed the value of our security precautions, and of good, swift communication with London.

3

Jean, meanwhile, was looking for an escape route through the Pyrenees. Operation 'Bonaparte', handling a mere fifteen or so evacuees a month, was a bit too slow.

Then word came to me, in Paris, that Henri Le Blais had got drunk in a St Brieuc café and started bragging that he belonged to the British Intelligence Service. When the same story reached me from London, I made for St Brieuc by the first train I could get on. Obviously he had not taken seriously my warning to keep his mouth shut.

It took ten hours to get to St Brieuc, which gave me time to cool off and think. I decided to go on to Plouha and see Le Cornec first. We had a long conversation, and agreed that Le Blais would have to be replaced. But I would dismiss him on the grounds that 'Bonaparte' had proved too dangerous and was not going to be repeated.

I met Le Blais in St Brieuc; and like the stupid fool he was, he had brought along his liaison agent to meet me. She was young, blonde and extremely good-looking; her name was Louisette Lorre. I told them of the abrupt stop put to 'Bonaparte', straightened accounts with him, and gave him a fair sum of money as a gratuity. He seemed perfectly satisfied.

When they left I followed the girl and asked her if she would come to work in Paris. She accepted and we made an appointment. She was to become my liaison agent. Louisette, I quickly discovered, was fearless to the point of rashness. She refused to kowtow to the *sales Boches*—a dangerous attitude to adopt in our position—and it was difficult to keep her in hand. But she proved invaluable to me.

4

I had other troubles at this time. One, which jeopardized the whole network, involved Ray's old boss, whose vanity and garrulousness had destroyed a previous organization and put Campinchi's life in danger. This lunatic, who was to become something of a hero after the war, had somehow escaped from the clutches of the Gestapo and had been given shelter by Campinchi in the suburbs of Paris.

Campinchi wanted me to ship him out via 'Bonaparte'. Knowing the man's reputation, I would have preferred to have nothing to do with him, but out of deference to both Campinchi and Ray, I agreed. It was an emotional decision, and one I bitterly regretted when we came to muster our parcels for the second 'Bonaparte', towards the end of February.

In the first place, this discredited big-shot turned up at Montparnasse with a former aide who was unknown to us, and had no business to be present at all, but had been told he could travel as far as St Brieuc. I was swallowing this when I discovered that Campinchi had given a farewell party for him the previous evening, to which he had invited a number of his Paris helpers. And this when I had spent so much time and effort insisting that members of the network should only meet in an emergency!

Worse was to come. On the train I came upon the precious pair carrying on a conversation *in English*, and smoking English cigarettes. By some miracle they were not reported; but at Plouha one of Le Cornec's guides reported that he had been followed by a stranger, whom he had managed to lose in the dark. I felt my months of work being eroded beneath my feet. I told Le Cornec that the stranger must be found.

At daybreak he sent out two men, armed with sten-guns, with the guide, to look for him. They duly picked him up, brought him to the farmhouse, and sent for me. I took a pistol, and there was murder in my heart. I found him trussed up on

159

a small bed in an outhouse under close guard—none other than the aide who was supposed to have gone home from St Brieuc. Big Shot had told him 'to hang around and he'd get him to England'.

He already knew too much about the network for comfort; but I put off killing him till I had had a chat with his former boss. I found him celebrating his imminent departure, and I swiftly put a damper on that party. Any more trouble from him, I said—and the gun was pointing at his heart and there was a round up the spout—and I should make short work of the pair of them. He knew I wouldn't hesitate—I was mad as hell —and I left him while I went away to think about it.

What riled me was that both Ray and Campinchi had acted behind my back, and had thereby put our operation at risk. I slept on it, and the next day I gave Ray a piece of my mind. He was suitably contrite. He had done excellent work for us, and I only wanted him to be more cautious in the future.

That night—26 February, 1944—we ran 'Bonaparte II'. Our number of parcels was up to twenty this time, among them our unwanted guest, and it went off without a hitch. A few days later London asked for a report on him—and they got one. I added that if they had it in mind to send him back to France, I would shoot him on sight, personally.

His wretched companion had been held prisoner at the farm. I told him enough to frighten him severely, and sent him packing. He would do us no harm, but he knew what would happen to him if he showed his face in Brittany again.

So, in spite of everything, our second evacuation went off successfully, and our score had risen to thirty-nine. It had given me a bad scare, and one bad disappointment. Two fighter pilots, one of them my first Canadian, got picked up by gendarmes on St Brieuc station, were handed over to the Germans, and ended up in a POW camp. To their everlasting credit, they never breathed a word about how they came to be at St Brieuc. By way of compensation, a British fighter pilot, shot down near Boulogne, was picked up by a post van, taken to St Brieuc, joined 'Bonaparte' and was back in England five days after he had left! No one could complain that we did not provide first-class service on occasion.

CHAPTER TEN

The Cross-Channel Ferry

1

IN Paris, Jean came to me with some good news. He had prospected in the south and found contraband experts who had taken some airmen across the Pyrenees. They were free to do so again.

Because, in the past, paying these men in advance had led to some double-crossing, I decided to give them the price they asked for before leaving, and promise to double it on the safe arrival of the airmen at the British Embassy in Madrid. I specified that we would check with Madrid by wireless.

Jean went back, got the guides to accept this arrangement, and brought some of them back with him. So, with all the loose ends tied up, the travelling back and forth began. Campinchi supplied only six of the airmen; the rest came from the north, through a fellow that I had met by chance.

It so happened that I knew the *concierge* of the Canadian Pacific building on the Boulevard des Capucines. He knew that I had something to do with airmen, for he had kept two of our parcels in the building for quite a while. One day he introduced me to a visitor from Beauvais, north of Paris. During the conversation it emerged that this man was stuck with a lot of airmen. He had, at one time, had a way out of France but it had broken down; now he had run out of money and had a number of hungry people on his hands. I arranged with him to send twenty-four airmen to Jean at Pau, where they would be taken to the foothills, ready for the journey to Spain.

By now I was becoming a real paymaster. I had four sections working for me and I was paying for the feeding of the evacuees, and the travelling and hotel expenses of all the workers; it amounted to a considerable sum.

But Shelburn was really getting into its stride now, and I intended to evacuate every airman that came down in France, for as long as we could stay out of Gestapo hands.

I had thought that rushing twenty-four airmen straight through Paris would relieve Campinchi, but in fact they were coming in from the north faster than he could empty his lodgings.

Jean reported that, altogether, almost thirty of them had gone through to Spain. Some had not been fit to travel and had had to be kept for the next trip. I sent him back with the money to pay the guides, with instructions to hang on a few days after they returned, supposedly awaiting news from Madrid. I had intended to check on the safe arrival of the parcels via London, but had been too busy to arrange it. The guides, however, were not to know this; and when they got their bonus they were raring to go again.

I wanted Jean to stay with the local people as much as possible, since his presence would give them confidence in us and in our ability to pay. They were inclined to regard us as fly-by-night northern strangers. In the meantime he was to set up another trip as soon as he could. He reckoned they could handle twice the previous number without any trouble.

The sky was full of Allied planes every night, and baled-out airmen were dropping all over the north of France. At one time Campinchi had seventy-five of them hidden in Paris, and found it difficult to supply them all with food and clothing. One chap, to his annoyance, arrived by train wearing flying boots; but as he took size fourteen it was understandable. Eventually a shoe-maker was found to make him some slippers.

I was trying to cut down my own work as it was urgent that I find more escape routes. I sometimes wondered whether I wouldn't end up having an airforce of my own in France.

I did not; but I did have what was known as the 'Channel Ferry Service'. I sent out a message to London telling them to put on 'Bonaparte' for 15, 19 and 23 March. They must have thought I had gone crazy, and asked for a repeat. I gave them the dates again, adding that the Royal Navy could do one every forty-eight hours so long as we were given due warning. The answer came back—agreed. So it was up to us.

It meant a considerable tightening up of our organization. So far, each departure had been arranged for a month ahead. Now we were proposing to put on three in nine days. One major change was that I briefed Campinchi and Le Cornec so that they could act directly from the BBC radio messages. These messages would regulate the flow of parcels from Paris to Brittany.

But having committed ourselves, we immediately ran into trouble. First the little train from St Brieuc to Plouha packed up, so we had to send the parcels to Châtelaudren and Guingamp, the next stops on the main line. At Châtelaudren, Le Cornec arranged for the local printer to loan his truck and driver to take them to Plouha, while at Guingamp the Resistance leader, Branchoux, received the parcels at the station and kept them until Le Cornec asked for them to be sent forward. Then they would be driven to Plouha at night by a garage man named Kérambrun, who had a small truck which he rented to the Germans in the daytime, and used for his own business at night. Part of his own business consisted of carting our parcels about. I have since met several American airmen who vividly remember riding around at night with the Jerries watching the roads.

Although it complicated matters to use two stations instead of one, we dared not risk so many strangers all arriving at a tiny place like Châtelaudren.

Ray and I went down in advance as usual, arriving in Guingamp on a bright morning. The first thing we saw was a convoy of nondescript vans going around the town at a snail's pace. We knew at once what they were doing—locating illicit broadcasters. We could spot them a mile away. Luckily Ray was not carrying a set as he had one in Plouha, so if there was a search, his luggage was clean. But that was only the beginning.

When we contacted Le Cornec, he told us that the whole coast was under an alert, nobody seemed to know why. Fishing boats and all other vessels were confined to their harbours under guard.

This was serious. It might be possible to get to Plouha and send out a message cancelling the operation, but it would be extremely hazardous. It would take me over an hour to code the message, and Ray would have to call London on emergency; and with the detector vans prowling round the Boche would be on to us at once. It would also attract their attention towards Plouha where a cargo of parcels was awaiting shipment.

It was too risky, and so instead I sent Ray back to Paris with instructions to try and cancel the second operation at least, even if it were too late to cancel the first. He had little enough time to do it, for the first one was timed for the following night.

I did not say anything to Le Cornec, but held my breath and hoped that the BBC message would put off the operation. Not a bit of it. When it came, it was confirmatory. There was nothing for it but to keep our fingers crossed and go ahead. The guides dispersed to muster the parcels and lead them to the cliff.

Down on the beach, I switched on the walkie-talkie that I had asked for, and which had arrived on the previous operation. At about the usual time the call came:

'Dinan!'

I waited a few seconds and answered:

'St Brieuc!'

They were right on time, about four miles away, and moving silently towards the shore. I signalled to Le Cornec that the men were to get ready, and there was much excited whispering among the evacuees as they squatted on the sand with their backs to the cliff.

Then there was an explosion, we could not tell where from; and another, this time out to sea. Over the phone came:

'We're being fired at. We'll have to pull out for the time being, but we'll be back.'

There were three or four more shots; but from seaward, only silence. There was nothing to do but wait.

'Do you think they'll come back?' one of the airmen whispered.

'Of course they'll come back,' I said, and wished I felt as confident as I tried to sound .

Two hours later, when my left arm was numb from holding the walkie-talkie to my ear, a faint noise came over it.

'Dinan!'

'St Brieuc!'

'Any trouble ashore?'

'None. How about you?'

'We're on our way back.'

'Any damage?'

'No. We should be inshore in half-an-hour.'

All was quiet and tense. We strained our ears, for the sound of the MTB, for the sound of oars, for more firing. Even the airmen stopped whispering, and all we could hear were the waves lapping on the beach.

Then, abruptly, out of the darkness the small boats appeared. It was getting late and we bundled the parcels aboard in double quick time.

As soon as they pulled away, we started to climb the cliff. I waited at the top with Le Cornec and sent the operators along with the incoming baggage. Le Cornec was listening for the sound of the MTB's engines, and he signalled that he could hear a low roar as they opened up. I passed on the information, and they slowed down. Dawn was just breaking.

When daylight came a few minutes later she was still visible, but well out and getting rapidly smaller. Mercifully, the Germans, after their earlier performance, must have been off-guard, for no shots followed her, and it seemed as if she had not been seen—which was just as well for us. This was confirmed next day when the Germans cancelled the alert.

I was sorry I had cancelled the second operation, but there

was still time to organize the third, and perhaps advance it a day or two. For this, however, I had to get back to Paris by the first train. Before leaving, I told Le Cornec that the second operation had probably been cancelled, but to be ready to carry it out if necessary.

4

In Paris I finally got in touch with Ray. He had not been able to send the first message, so everything remained as originally planned, which was fine. I could have got back to Brittany by the 19th, but I was worn out with travelling and badly needed a rest. So instead, I sent Louisette, whom Le Cornec knew, to warn him that the second operation was going ahead.

Anyway, there was work to be done in Paris, for with so much happening, Campinchi was having a merry old time with his guides. Some of the most reliable could not get away for all three operations for fear of losing their jobs, for which one could hardly blame them. We made things as easy as possible, but this did not alter the fact that on the journey to Brittany they had to stay with their parcels, which meant they were up all night. They had reserved seats, and were put up at hotels in Guingamp, and then took the night train back to Paris, possibly to take out a new convoy straight away. As we did not like a guide to handle more than two or three parcels at a time, it meant a lot of going back and forth.

But Campinchi was having to saddle them with four or even five. This was madness, but, as he said, it was the only way he could meet the quota, which had now escalated to twenty-five per operation.

Louisette came back to report that the second operation had gone off without incident, and we rejoiced; fifty parcels had reached England in a week. Ray and I moved down to Plouha and stayed with Francis Baudet at his mother-in-law's place at St Bartholémy, a mile or so away. Madame Le Saux was a widow, and pleased to have friends of her son-in-law to stay, despite the fact that she was already putting up his family. She had a large and comfortable house and was extremely hospitable.

Almost at once we ran into the sort of difficulty that was inevitable, working at such high pressure. One of the guides from Paris, Massenet (who now lives in Montreal), had arrived in Châtelaudren with seven parcels trailing along behind him. The train was three hours late, and there was no one to meet him. Luckily it was market day and he had managed to mingle with the crowds until he could get his convoy out of the town. He had made discreet enquiries of a café owner, who had referred him to the printer. The printer had said: 'This is a matter for Léon,'—though he was not supposed to know me by that name—and phoned Le Cornec, who, in turn, had phoned Francis, and Francis bicycled off with his sister-in-law to sort it out.

This sort of risk was unavoidable. We had been lucky so far, and we knew it; it was a relief when the third consecutive operation went off as scheduled. This meant that we had successfully shipped out seventy-five useful fighting men in eight days; no wonder London were referring to us as the Cross-Channel Ferry Service!

CHAPTER ELEVEN

Exits and Entrances

1

As a result of this intense activity, Shelburn was in a turmoil. It was high time to slow down and straighten things out. Anyway, we had just about cleaned out Paris and the north of quickly available parcels. More would soon start to filter through as we were getting well known. That was where the danger lay; we were too well known and the Gestapo might easily hear about us.

We were already past the point when we could reasonably expect to have been in enemy hands. But there was no sense in brooding on that. All we could do was push ahead; and we still badly needed an alternative exit route. It was the search for one that led me to Captain Dréau. He was a staunch member of the Resistance in the area south-west of Brest, and knew exactly what was going on in that region.

The plan for 'Austerlitz', as I christened it, was to ship the parcels out in a fishing boat, rendezvous with a British ship forty or fifty miles out, and transfer them. After that the French vessel would go fishing in the normal way. It had been done before, twice successfully. The third time they were caught, and eighteen fishermen were shot by the Germans.

With Pierre Dréau I went and had a careful look at Concarneau, where trawlers still went out to the fishing grounds every day. The harbour was under constant watch by the Germans, and the men would have to be smuggled on board at dead of night. But that was only the start. The trawlers were invariably searched by the German customs before leaving port. Hiding fifteen men on a trawler was not going to be easy, but I thought I had a feasible plan.

Before going out, the trawlers went to the ice factory and filled up the after-hold with ice. If we made a large box in the centre of the hold, got the men into it, and covered it up with ice, there was every chance our vessel would pass the inspection. Once at sea, they could be released.

In theory it should have been possible; but there were too many risks. Other fishermen would see the work going on aboard the trawler, the men at the ice factory would see the box in the hold, and if there were any delay, our charges would suffocate or freeze—so I had to abandon the idea.

And, of course, always at the back of everyone's mind was the knowledge that eighteen men had been shot trying exactly the same thing, and the Germans were on the alert.

We were forced to consider an operation similar to 'Bonaparte' but from somewhere in south Brittany; but a suitable beach was hard to find, and the navy considered it too far from base. Undeterred, Captain Dréau and I bicycled the entire coastline, from Pointe de Penmarch to Quiberon, talking to the local fishermen, inspecting every bay and cove; but we failed to find anywhere that was really suitable.

There was one other possibility I had looked into and for which I had plans under the name of 'Waterloo'. To me, by now more French than Canadian, it had an ominous ring about it. The plan was a variation on 'Austerlitz', and consisted in taking our parcels out to sea ourselves in small boats and putting them aboard a British fishing boat which would be waiting a few miles offshore.

The place chosen was L'Aber-Wrach, on the north-west corner of Brittany, which had already been the scene of one disaster. The previous December, when the Royal Navy had refused to come for 'Bonaparte', they had also rejected an alternative at L'Aber-Wrach. Certain Frenchmen, scornful of the navy's seamanship, had attempted to put the operation on themselves. But the boats had been swamped and hurled on to the rocks, and a dozen or more airmen had been drowned. So, reluctantly, 'Waterloo' also had to be abandoned.

2

To digress for a moment, I had reason to get to know two of the survivors from that disaster rather too well. After being rescued they were taken back to Paris and lodged in some style near the Trocadéro, in the Avenue du Président Wilson.

Campinchi told me about them. Apparently they were British, and had rejected all offers of repatriation. I decided I had better go and have a word with them, so I went round to the apartment and rang the bell. A uniformed maid opened the door. I stepped forward and said:

'I would like to see the two airmen, please.'

'Airmen? I don't know anything about airmen,' she said.

I pushed my way past her and into the dining room, with her clutching at my arm and clucking like a hen. At the table was madame, with a man on either side of her and a spare place laid, presumably for the maid. It was not difficult to see why they were in no hurry to leave, more particularly as I gathered that madame was passionately devoted to one of them, and the maid to the other.

As I broke in, the woman at the table rose in wrath, demanding to know the reason for the intrusion. I disregarded her and spoke to the men in English.

'I am Captain Harrison of the British Intelligence Service. Stand up when an officer is talking to you!'

They did, and said, 'Sir.'

When I taxed them with their refusal to budge, they protested that they did not want to try and swim the Channel again. I laid down the law.

'You'd better be ready to leave tonight, or I'll personally see that you cross the Channel under arrest and stand court martial.'

'We'll be ready, sir!' And they were.

There were touching scenes that evening when the time for departure came; but I was standing across the street, where they could see me, and the ladies' tears proved ineffective in the face of a flesh-and-blood member of British Intelligence. But who could blame the ladies, or the boys? It was much nicer to forget about the war. Even I had some pangs about breaking up this comfortable *ménage,* but what the hell! We were at war, and the Germans were not letting us forget it.

3

Jean Mettling had brought back from the south, in a loaf of bread, the plans of the German defences of the city of Montpellier. Information was not in our line, but this had been dropped in our laps and we might just as well send it off to London.

It was now Jean's turn to get into trouble. Le Blais started it by babbling again. I thought that I could scare him into leaving Brittany, so I sent Jean, who was an Alsatian and spoke French with a German accent, to Plouha to make an indiscreet investigation on him. Jean would be taken for a Gestapo agent, and that should be enough to put the wind up M Le Blais, I thought. Jean travelled, as we all did, on false papers made out by our printer. When he got to Plouha, he went to a certain restaurant that I had described to him and started asking questions about Le Blais. Ten minutes later the local *gendarmes* arrived on the scene and asked him for his identification. His papers said that he was from the same small village as one of the *gendarmes,* so they arrested him.

The next day I arrived in Plouha, and Le Cornec, very pleased with himself, told me that a German agent had come along and asked questions about Le Blais. He had immediately sent out Dagorne, one of the local *gendarmerie,* and his partner Garion, to cramp his syle. Dagorne was to lock up the pro-German under any excuse, while Le Blais was warned to get out fast. He was trying to protect not Le Blais but the network, which might receive some unwelcome attention if the Germans heard about us.

Dagorne, who had expected his prisoner to get in touch with his superiors, was very surprised that he expressed no desire to contact the Gestapo at St Brieuc.

I was stunned by this development. My ruse had worked all

171

right, for Le Blais had gone; but I had set off a comedy of errors which suddenly took a serious turn. As we gave the *gendarmerie* orders, there should not have been any problem about arranging Jean's release, but when I told Le Cornec that the prisoner was really working for Shelburn and should be let go, it was his turn to be stunned. Jean had been taken to the main *gendarmerie* in St Brieuc, where we had no contacts at all.

To reassure him that he was not forgotten, I sent Louisette to see him in the guise of his fiancée. As he did not know her, the moment the cell door was opened, she threw her arms about his neck, kissed him and whispered:

'I have come from Lucien.'

Jean, smart fellow, caught on at once, returned the embrace, and eagerly accepted the cigarettes and other delicacies she had brought him.

In the meantime, Le Cornec had contacted somebody at the *gendarmerie* at St Brieuc, as well as the judge, so that when Jean came up for trial on a charge of false identity, which was a serious offence, he was released on conditional liberty. That was all we needed.

4

After our series of three successful March operations I received a message from London. It took me forty-five minutes to decipher, but it was worth the effort. It read:

HEARTIEST CONGRATULATIONS FROM DIRECTOR OF MILITARY INTELLIGENCE ON RECENT SEA OPERATIONS STOP YOUR HAZARDOUS WORK FULLY APPRECIATED ESPECIALLY IN VIEW OF PRESENT LARGE SCALE TIGHTENING UP BY ENEMY STOP THANKS FOR CONTACT ADDRESS STOP PLEASE GIVE US PASSWORD TO BE USED STOP GOOD LUCK FOR THE FUTURE END

And just to show that they really appreciated the work we were doing, they had promoted both Ray and me to Lieutenant. The next message said that I appeared in the Canadian Gazette as a captain. This was timely as in Paris I had been passing myself off as a captain and Ray as a lieutenant. It was a question of prestige, as the French people attach more importance to rank than we do. I had informed London of my presumption, and they had made it good.

CHAPTER TWELVE

Arabs, Sailors and a Belgian Ace

1

In April we put on another operation from Plouha, our sixth. In the event, it was a routine affair; but beforehand, because of the firing on the previous occasion, London had objected that Plouha was burnt-out as a departure point. We had used it too much. I pointed out that I was on the spot and thus in a better position to judge than they were.

They conceded the point, there was no trouble, and twenty-three fighting men were returned safely to their units. Among them was one 'Leo the Belgian', a fighter pilot from the RAF who had come down north of Paris. He had the highest possible opinion of himself and was completely undisciplined. After hauling him out of a café in Guingamp, where he had got drunk and started talking out of turn, I had to put him under arrest. He was finally embarked bound hand and foot and gagged with adhesive tape. Two of the guides were appointed to hold him; and for good measure, one had a heavy stick to hit him over the head with, and the other a sharp knife. It was the only time he did not give any trouble—but that was hardly surprising.

London asked me for a report on him, and told me to pay his debts. I replied that they could come over and pay them themselves, I had more important things to do than play nurse-maid to a drunkard. I heard no more.

174

Immediately after this operation the Germans started to lay a minefield along the top of the cliff. It was fifty yards wide, and they used all kinds of explosives, including old French navy shells of heavy calibre, complete with booby traps. I was told about it when I was in Paris and came back right away, bringing along a pair of good binoculars.

All day long, Pierre Huet, Job Mainguy and Marie-Thérèse watched from behind bushes and recorded the exact place where each mine was laid. At night, when the Germans had left, they went in and marked a path through them. We knew more about that minefield than the Germans themselves. To be on the safe side, I had two mine detectors sent in from London; but during the next operation, Huet and Mainguy went over during the evening and marked each mine with a white cloth. As soon as it was over they picked up the markers as they left.

We had another operation the following month; but before it I had to go back to Guingamp to screen two parcels brought in from the countryside. They were an odd pair. They looked like Arabs, spoke only a few words of French but understood some German. I tried my scraps of Arabic on them without success; but then they came out with the word 'India', and after a lot of palavering and sign language, I gathered that they had come from India in the first days of the war, and had been in France ever since.

The story rang true, but it had to be checked. It occurred to me that any soldier in the British Army had to know words of command in English, however little of the language he spoke, so, sending one of them out of the room, I put the other through a short exercise of standard drill—'Attention', 'Stand at Ease', and so forth. He obeyed correctly and without hesitation. Then I gave him a broomstick and made him do arms drill. Again he passed, and so did his companion when his turn came. Both had definitely been in the British army, and they were accepted. Later I heard that they had been made prisoners by the Germans in 1939, and had escaped three times. While they were free, they passed themselves off as North Africans. One could only imagine what a rough time they must have had during those four years.

This little game of screening doubtful people was easier than it might sound. From the first word they spoke, we started to try and identify their accents, and we became surprisingly good at it with practice. At the same time, a man's accent had to tally with his story. An American with a cockney accent, for example, or a Canadian with a Texan accent had some explaining to do.

Then there was the fellow who refused to give anything but his name, rank and number, in the manner approved for a prisoner-of-war. This was no use to us; we wanted to know his squadron, what sort of aircraft he had been flying, who his companions were—information we could check with London if necessary. If he persisted in his refusal, we would ask him if he took us for enemies, because if he did, he was perfectly free to go. This usually did the trick.

3

The Resistance leader, Branchoux, who belonged to the network, was always trying to increase his self-esteem by inviting me to meet other members of clandestine organizations. The first was the supposed chief of the secret army in France; then it was an agent of the British Intelligence Service who was in Brittany and wanted help. I refused. I did not like meeting strangers, no matter who they were; and if they were BIS, which I doubted, it was up to them either to send a message to London, or, if they couldn't do that, to send us the coded message for forwarding. London would then tell us to pick them up and identify them.

Then, one day, Le Cornec and I were walking past a small hotel in Guingamp, when he said:

'This is the place where Branchoux's "agent" is hiding out. Do you want to meet him?'

I hesitated, but he assured me that the hotel-keeper was a friend and there was little danger of a trap, so I told him to get us some weapons and we would pay him a surprise visit.

There were only two men in the hall; they turned round to inspect us. Le Cornec and I both had our pistols half-drawn. I looked at the men, and nearly fell over backwards with surprise. One of them was a soldier from my own battalion, Robert Vanier. He was just as amazed as I was. Le Cornec was no less taken aback to see me throw my arms round a complete stranger and hug him! After the hand-shaking and back-slapping came the introductions and the questions. The other man, who was a Breton, watched the reunion impassively.

Robert, like myself, had been captured on the Dieppe raid, but had later escaped with three other *Fusiliers Mont-Royal* and made his way back to England. While I had gone off to Africa, he had volunteered, with Conrad Lafleur, one of his companions, for MI9. He had been in France for some time; indeed, he was in the network that was supposed to receive us on that first abortive flight when we had been forced to turn back.

Robert and Conrad were both radio operators; but Conrad was working in northern France. Robert had lost his radio and had no code of his own—a precaution I had insisted on with Ray—and had mentioned to Branchoux that he was a member of BIS. Branchoux, true to character, had promised to get him to England. Robert was incredulous when I told him I would have him back in England in less than twenty-four hours. What he did not know was that a 'Bonaparte' operation was scheduled for that very night.

Just before this, an extraordinary thing had happened. One of my operators, Jean Trihiou, had become too well known to the Boche, and I sent him out in February. Jean, who was a local farmer, was a member of Le Cornec's group, and had been one of the operators for the first 'Bonaparte' in January. Thus he knew the beach and the countryside like his own cow-yard.

London had trained him for sabotage work and sent him back in charge of two other men; and, arguing that he knew the area so well, hadn't bothered to tell us to meet them. What neither they nor Jean knew, however, was that during his absence the Germans had laid that minefield.

The three of them landed at dead of night, climbed the cliff and walked straight through it without touching off a mine. It was only later that we learned of Jean's return.

But that was not the end of the story. The small boat which landed the party was commanded by Lieutenant Guy Hamilton, RN, who, as was usual among landing officers, spoke French like a native. He had two sailors with him.

Hamilton had orders to inspect the beaches in the vicinity, which he did; but he took longer than had been allowed, and as they rowed back towards the MTB, they heard it pulling away. They were stranded.

They rowed back to the shore and found a cave where they hid their weapons and the oars. Then the boat was half-filled with stones, and pushed out as far as it would go, where it sank.

They had no food or drinking water, and did not know where to go, so they climbed the cliff and hid on the edge of a copse. After thirty-six hours they saw a small boy. Guy Hamilton hailed him and asked him if he knew anybody in the Resistance. As it happened he did not; but he knew someone even more useful, Marie-Thérèse, and he went off to fetch her.

When she heard the story, she realized that it could be true, for she knew Jean Trihiou well, and had been there to see him off to England. She told them to stay put while she went for food and water. Then she reported to Le Cornec, who fetched them after dark and took them to a friendly farmhouse, and then sent a message to me in Paris.

I checked the story as soon as I arrived, and sent someone to the cave to recover the weapons and other gear. The next day a message came in through Ray, telling me to try and pick up a British naval officer and two ratings who were stranded on the coast. My acknowledgement was to the effect that Shelburn did not neglect its duties; too bad London were always a few days late. The Royal Navy would get a free passage on the next operation and lodging in the meantime at our expense. I also mentioned that we were giving Robert Vanier and his friend a free ticket. It was a sly pleasure, having the chance of pulling London's leg.

During the return trip to Paris after this incident, the train I was on was heavily bombed and machine-gunned. Although there were several near misses, the damage was not serious, and we were a mere six hours late—time to appreciate the irony of the situation. Here was I, risking my neck and worse to help Allied airmen escape; and they were no sooner back in England than they came and shot up my train!

At this period of the war, when the Allied air offensive was mounting to its D-Day crescendo, the railway system was a primary target. The Germans, having no airforce to defend it, took to mixing freight and passenger wagons, with ack-ack guns mounted on trucks between. Freight trains alone were a pet target of Allied fighter-bombers, and it was quite common for the pilots to fly over once in order to give the crew time to bale out; then they blew up the locomotive. If the train was known to be carrying ammunition, however, there would be no warning run, and that train would not get very far. The Germans took to travelling at night, and the railwaymen would give advance warning. Then the saboteurs would have a merry old time pulling up the tracks.

The Germans tried sending a patrol locomotive ahead; but the saboteurs simply let it go, and then blew up the ammunition train behind it. Petrol tankers, treated in this manner, really made a nice bonfire.

It was now late May, and although the French knew nothing about the coming invasion, London was sending across plenty of explosives and weapons, with instructions on how to hit the Boche where it hurt, and large numbers of trained saboteurs.

There were more and more searches at railway stations. Ray and I often had to carry dangerous luggage, so we developed a system to avoid being caught. One of us went ahead, carrying a harmless case, while the other stayed by the train. If the scout did not return, the incriminating bag would be checked in at the left luggage counter, to be recovered when the coast was clear.

CHAPTER THIRTEEN

'Roger Le Légionnaire'

1

WHEN I was in Paris, I continued to live in the apartment in Avenue Charles Floquet. Louisette, who was my liaison agent, moved in as well, but our relationship, whatever the reader may suppose, was platonic and professional.

The *concierge* assumed—and told all the other tenants—that I was a highly successful black market operator. That was all right; but then Louisette heard that our charwoman was telling everyone that I was a British General, no less. I suppose I should have been flattered at my promotion; instead I asked Louisette to try and find out what she was playing at.

It turned out that she was one of those odd people who invent stories, presumably to enhance their own importance; so, not only was I a senior British officer in disguise, but she was secretary to a German Colonel. We knew that she worked for a German Colonel, who, like several other German officers, lived in the building, but she certainly could not have been his secretary. In the first place she would have had to be German; secondly, she wasn't educated enough to be anybody's secretary.

I didn't worry too much about her tattling, as any serious investigator would soon find out that she was a romancer; all the same, it was annoying to discover that I was being associated with the British, if only in the fantasies of an imaginative char.

Agents normally spent a maximum of six months behind the enemy lines; now time was up for Ray and me, and London was calling us back. I was most unwilling to go, for a whole host of reasons. Quite apart from the fact that new men wouldn't be as efficient as we were for some time, we were not under suspicion—or at least we had seen no signs of it. Our nerves were standing up well, we did not suffer from anxiety, and most important of all, our Shelburn organization was working well. It would be a terrible wrench to leave all our staunch and loyal team to carry on; we would feel as if we were deserting them.

I had to let Ray make his own decision. We met in the morning, as was usual after the reception of a message, to exchange information.

'London are recalling us,' I said.

'Yippee! When are we leaving?'

'You'll be leaving by the next Bonaparte operation if they can send a replacement by then.'

'What about you?'

I shook my head. 'I'm staying on.'

Ray started thinking hard. After thirty seconds, he said:

'Well, if you're staying, so am I.'

'Good,' and we shook hands on it.

To hell with London and their reliefs; we didn't need anybody.

2

Ray had been having quite a time with his transmissions, because the electricity was being cut throughout most of the city in the daytime. He had three wireless sets in Paris, hidden in different districts to avoid having to carry them around, and for every message he changed sectors to avoid the possibility of the Germans' locating him.

Once, when there was German interference while he was receiving, he immediately warned London, went off the air, and then changed sector. It was the only way to throw them off the scent.

In my district, however, because there were a lot of German officers living there and the important École Militaire, occupied by the Boche, was close by, the electricity stayed on day and night. If the worst came to the worst, Ray would have to operate from my apartment.

The worst soon happened, and he arranged a rendezvous with London for two o'clock in the morning. I had a friend, Odette, staying with me* and she knew Ray was a friend of mine. All the same she was surprised one night to find him in the apartment getting drunk on Grand-Marnier.

After a time she went to bed. She would have been even more surprised if she had come back into the living room a little later on. Ray, instead of sprawling half drunk on the couch, was up on a chair fixing the aerial, and right on schedule he was on the air. Next morning he was bleary-eyed and full of apologies for his sottish behaviour. This procedure was repeated several times, and Odette never discovered what antics my 'drunken friend' got up to in her absence.

3

In Brittany we had had some trouble from a Gestapo agent who was known at that time as *Roger le Légionnaire*. I was out to get him; and when word was brought to me that he was working near Blois, between Orleans and Tours, I sent Jean down to see what he could find out.

After a time, Jean duly reported back. To begin with, as was only to be expected, Roger was using a different name. Gestapo agents changed names every time they changed districts, just as we did ourselves. They did not like to be known, any more than we did, for we could kill them just as fast as they could arrest us; and in any case, a known agent is useless. They were normally French, or people who could pass as French. An agent with even a trace of a German accent had to keep in the background and only emerge from the shadows for a swoop.

Jean's report was characteristically thorough. The pattern he succeeded in tracing was, briefly, as follows:

1. Mauger, a jeweller, formerly Mayor of Blois, fled in March, 1943, and reports that:

* We later got married!

2. John Picksgill, a Canadian officer, was arrested and interrogated by:
3. Ludwig Bauer, a German officer of the *Sicherheitspolizei* of Blois. Bauer had a mistress:
4. Mona 'La Blonde', whose real name is:
5. Marie-Delphine Reiminger, born at Metz in 1906; speaks German as is to be expected from an Alsatian; used to be known as:
6. Mme Blavot, at Dijon, in 1939; holds a doctor's degree in French literature, but this does not prevent her from having loose morals; arrested three times for swindling; is intelligent, blustering and sensual. She started working for the Germans in 1940 as an interpreter at the *Kommandantur* in Metz.

Jean recognized her in the company of the *Feldkommandant* of Blois, Colonel Hipe, and followed her to a restaurant and accosted her, using the common accent as a pretext. After a few days of meetings he took her to bed. Mona liked men and was given to boasting. According to her, she and Roger were responsible for Picksgill's arrest, and for a raid on a British Intelligence network in Paris in June, 1943. They also worked together on the arrests of the chiefs of the CNR network at Caluire, on 21 June 1943.*

I decided to deal with Roger first, since he was more energetic and enterprising, as well as being an accredited agent of the Gestapo, while she was only a helper.

Jean had discovered where he kept his car in Blois. It was a public garage, and Jean's plan was to buy himself a bicycle and store it in the same place—this was a common French practice—and, when the opportunity arose, attach a plastic grenade, which I gave him, to the car. If everything went well, *Roger le Légionnaire* would blow himself up.

The execution proved more difficult, for Jean soon found that he always kept his car locked. Jean waited for several days. Then one evening he noticed that a rear window had been left open a few inches, and he managed to unlock the door. Quickly

* Mona was arrested at the Liberation and condemned to twenty years by a Court of Justice at Dijon. She was sent to prison in Romorantin.

taking the cap off the grenade, he unrolled the tape that held the pin, attached the grenade beneath the dashboard, and pulled the pin out. The trap was set. The least shock or swerve of the car would be enough to dislodge the grenade so that it landed on the floor right between the driver's feet, and exploded.

Jean waited all the following day, but Roger did not come for his car. The next morning he was hardly installed in a café over the way when the car came out of the garage, driven by somebody else, a younger man who worked with Roger. He did not get far. Almost as soon as he turned into the street, the grenade exploded. The car swerved to the right, climbed the pavement and hit a tree.

Jean was one of the first across the street. All the windows of the car had been blown out, and the man lay back against the seat, unconscious. He was bleeding from eyes, ears, nose and mouth. His trouser-legs were torn right off, and his legs were blasted and bleeding.

A few days later Jean came back to report. Roger and Mona had disappeared, probably taking the attack on their friend as a warning. I reckoned that the driver of the car would have been killed, for the concussion grenade, though not containing any shrapnel, would have a shattering effect in a closed car. Nothing had appeared in the local newspapers about this 'accident'.

We had missed Roger by sheer bad luck, but I was not displeased with the results of Jean's investigation. Roger and Mona would lie low for a while, and other members of the Gestapo would be watching out for their own skins. The fact that there were no reprisals on the French population meant that the dead man was French. His death was a matter for the French police, and some of their inspectors would be as blind as could be.

While he was in Blois, Jean had made contact with the local Resistance, and they would look out for any news of Roger. We would attend to him later.

4

On the morning of 6 June, as I had nothing particularly pressing to do, after a shave and breakfast, I switched on the radio for the news. It was eleven o'clock, and there was a special announcement:

'Early this morning the Allies landed in Normandy.'

It was followed by the usual propaganda, but this time there was a slight variation:

'They will be thrown back into the sea.'

Excitement thrilled through me. At long last it had come! I knew that this was no Dieppe; this time it was the real thing.*

The next day a message came in from London:

'Get to Brittany and stay there.'

This meant that they intended to cut off the Brittany peninsula, and we had better be behind the Allied lines. But getting to Brittany was more easily said than done.

* A lot of people have asked me if I had advance warning of the invasion. The answer is no. The first I knew of it was from the radio announcement; though, as I mentioned earlier, I had guessed it was coming by the type and quantity of stores brought in via 'Bonaparte'.

CHAPTER FOURTEEN

Free Lift to St Brieuc

1

FOR the previous month or so a good part of the Allied air forces had been paying particular attention to the French railway system. The main junctions and marshalling yards of north-western France had been the target for many tons of bombs; bridges had been blown up; and airfields were being regularly and thoroughly strafed.

On my last trip to Brittany, the rail-yard at Trappes had been bombed the day before. It was a shambles, craters everywhere and locomotives up on end. Ours had been the first train to crawl through; but according to the official news, the yard had suffered only slight damage from a near miss while the town, across the road from it, had suffered heavily. This version of events did not correspond with what I could see from the coach window. There appeared to be some damage to the town, but not much.

As a result of this savage intervention by the Air Force, there were only two ways of getting to Brittany since the landing, on foot or by bicycle. The latter was the quicker; and so Louisette, Ray and I all equipped ourselves with bikes. Mine, bought at black market prices, was a monstrously heavy machine, and pedalling it was like shifting a five-ton truck.

We left Paris early in the morning of 11 June. Louisette travelled in front, with Ray close behind her to keep an eye on her, while I brought up the rear. I kept well back so that I would appear to be totally unconnected with them. They had plenty of cash, enough, in fact, to carry on the network, should anything happen to me.

Everything seemed in order except myself. I was suffering from a severe attack of boils on my posterior; two in particular were situated right between my legs, where the saddle chafed them with every push. However, an old soldier cannot stop for such minor details. I was well off: at least I didn't have to march. In any case it was all my own fault if I was suffering from boils. Since I had been in France I had been living well and neglecting to take much exercise. Now I was paying for it.

We had quite a trip in front of us—over 400 miles on roads that were far from safe. Allied fighter-bombers patrolled them day and night and strafed everything that moved, and were hardly likely to hold their fire for three bicycles.

We came to Trappes, where no attempt had been made to repair the damage. The Germans were busy elsewhere, and the French had given up, reasoning that whatever they did, it would be blown to smithereens again as soon as it was mended. There was not a single track, out of the twenty or twenty-five, that was not cut in four or five places. Box cars were piled two and three high.

The Germans were constantly telling the French population that they were pushing the Allied forces back into the sea; but to me it looked quite the other way round. This opinion had been reinforced the previous Sunday, in Paris, when I had seen heavy tanks heading for Normandy on their own tracks. Only dire necessity would cause anyone to bring up heavy tanks that way over 200 miles of paved roads. Whatever they chose to say, the Germans were in trouble.

By lunch-time on that day we were halfway to Chartres; not bad going with a stiff wind against us. We had found a bakery with some hot bread, a grocery still selling food and some wine, so we picnicked by the roadside. Remounting afterwards was a refinement of torture.

We reached Chartres in good time and found a boarding house for the night. The proprietress was a talkative woman from, of all places, Quebec; and throughout dinner she regaled us with information about Canada in general and Quebec in particular. We played the part of interested Frenchmen, curious about the strange ways of the new world across the Atlantic. She even went so far as to describe the Dieppe raid, and mentioned agents from BIS who travelled about France quite freely.

When we set out again the following morning, we could hear bombing ahead of us. We came to a long hill. Halfway up we dismounted to walk the rest of the way—and suddenly we heard the sound of planes from over the crest. We pulled the bicycles off the road and crouched in the ditch as three aircraft shot past low over our heads. They were Lightnings, and they had come over the hill so fast I doubted whether they had seen us.

They turned for another run, and we clung close to a small stone wall that bordered a steep slope to our right. The Lightnings were not interested in us, but in something on the other side of the wall. We peered over. Down in the valley was a railway station, with two freight trains stopped there.

The aircraft appeared to take a leisurely look at them, then flew away in a long, shallow turn, to give the French plenty of time to get away. From our grandstand view we could see tiny figures running away from the tracks. Then the aircraft returned and machine-gunned the trains and the station. Again they banked round, and on their second run dropped their bombs, flew on and disappeared, leaving a shambles behind them.

All along the road after that were similar scenes of destruction: a burnt-out German truck, or a crater where an ammunition-carrier had blown up, its bits scattered over the nearby fields. Every 200 yards or so there were slit-trenches for the protection of truck-drivers, but they hadn't always had time to get to them.

All that day we pedalled steadily on. At one point we came to a bridge that had been blown up, but a farmer rowed us across the river in his boat. Some twenty miles before Laval we found a stream behind a farmhouse and went in for a swim. I needed that badly as my boils were getting worse. The farmer also let us have some food and wine.

When we hit the road again, it was about four o'clock in the afternoon. We were free-wheeling downhill towards a large river when aircraft came over to bomb the bridge, so we sat down and watched the show. Time and again they tried to hit it, and failed. Eventually, after one near miss, they sheered off in disgust. We took our chance and nipped across before they came back.

In the suburbs of Laval a local school had been turned into a reception centre. When the woman in charge saw me getting off my bicycle she asked whether I had been wounded. I had, but only in my pride. I told her of my condition and she sent off for a nurse. In the meantime we were given a splendid meal, which I found it more convenient to eat standing up. Afterwards the nurse dressed my 'wounds' and I felt better. Cots had been set up in the classrooms, and we had a good night's sleep.

2

The following morning we rode on to Rennes. It was about 50 miles, and we were there for lunch. The pain, which was acute when I started, gradually eased until it was just about bearable.

We were now on the last lap to St Brieuc. We had about seventy-five miles to go and we wanted to make it before nightfall. In spite of everything, the journey was going well. Then, just after we had crossed a small bridge, a German sergeant by the side of the road yelled at me to halt. I was in the rear, as usual, and paid no attention.

He shouted again, and this time he drew his revolver. I was fifteen yards away by then, and I doubted whether he could hit me. I stood on my pedals to sprint off, when he yelled at a soldier next to him. This fellow brought up his rifle and aimed at me. This was a very different matter; he could hardly miss, so I dismounted and waited.

They both came up to me and the sergeant motioned that he wanted my bicycle. I hung on to the handlebars and refused to let go. I knew that he had no right to requisition it. There was a *Feldgendarme* sergeant sitting on the curb some distance back, and I shouted at him:

'*Feldgendarme, Feldgendarme!*'

He came running up, fastening the chain of his breastplate around his neck as he ran. This was his badge of office and he would have no authority without it. He spoke French, and I explained to him what was happening, protesting vehemently that the other sergeant had no right to take my bicycle. I could see him hesitating, but at that moment, Louisette and Ray, who had seen what was going on and had hidden their machines in an alley-way, came back. A little crowd had gathered and were fulminating against the Germans. Above their voices came Louisette's:

'*Bande de vaches!*' she said loudly.

The *Feldgendarme* understood her clearly enough; he let out a shocked:

'*Mademoiselle!*'

I grabbed Louisette by the shoulder and pushed her out of the crowd. I whispered:

'Get away from here, you'll have us all in jail.'

With this I gave her a shove and pretended to kick her for good measure.

The *Feldgendarme* took this to be vindication of his honour but he wasn't in a mood to let me win the argument. Between them the two sergeants stripped the bicycle of my things, which they handed back to me, and wrote me out a receipt for it.

I gave my baggage to Ray and Louisette to take with them to St Brieuc, and told them to press on. I would get there somehow—and in time for my appointment in Yffiniac the following afternoon. I managed to sound confident, but in truth I had not the faintest idea how I was going to get there. I certainly could not walk it in the time; besides, if I were out after curfew, I would be picked up by the Germans. We were getting near the fighting zone, and they would be a lot stricter.

I sat on the curb for a while, feeling dejected and at a loss. Then an idea struck me. They had no right to take my bicycle; therefore I would go to the German authorities, lodge a complaint, and demand that they transport me to St Brieuc.

In my pockets were the same identity papers that I had used at Pont-l'Abbé, those of Jean-François Guillou, stone-mason contractor, working for the Germans. I made my way to the *Standortkommandantur*. A sentry at the door examined my papers carefully and told me that I should see a Major von Müller. He handed my papers over to a picket who escorted me to the major's office and gave them to him.

While I was waiting in the corridor, I could hear an argument going on between an angry and voluble Frenchman and a very calm German officer who spoke good French with hardly a trace of an accent.

When my turn came, I too was an angry and voluble Frenchman. I pounded the desk and complained bitterly that German soldiers had stolen my bicycle. Was it my fault, I demanded, if the English decided to invade while I was on a business trip to Paris? I had observed Maréchal Pétain's advice to co-operate with the occupying forces and this was what I got in return. I really let him have it.

He begged me to calm down. Unfortunately he had no bicycle to give away, but the captain of the *Feldgendarmerie*, he was sure, would look after me. In very tolerable French, he was, as they say, passing the buck.

I was escorted to the captain. Their security was good; nobody was allowed to roam around unaccompanied, and they held on to one's papers until one was led out. The major was courteous, for his job was dealing with civilians. The captain, to whom I was taken next, was a police officer and very stiff.

He spoke no French, and I claimed not to understand German, so an interpreter was called for. When he had heard my story, he sent for the *Feldgendarmerie* sergeant.

The sergeant appeared and stood rigidly to attention in front of him. When he discovered that my story was true, he flew into a rage and called the sergeant every kind of fool and *Dummkopf*, plus several other names new to me. Once I thought he was going to strike him; the sergeant remained motionless.

The captain turned to me:

'You will be reimbursed in full.'

I had told them I paid 11,000 francs for the cycle.

'11,000 francs won't get me to St Brieuc,' I said, 'find me another bicycle and I'll gladly pay whatever you ask.'

Unfortunately he had no bicycle either, at any price.

'All right,' I said, 'then get me to St Brieuc.'

He almost fell over backwards. He, a captain of the *Feldgendarmerie*, transporting French civilians in German army vehicles? Preposterous!

After a lot of arguing, he finally agreed. With an ill grace he signed a transportation order, and gave instructions to the sergeant to see that I was given transport. Perhaps he was afraid I might take the matter further. It had been, after all, a case of outright theft by the sergeant of the *Artillerie*.

So my papers were returned to me and I was taken back to the crossroads to await a vehicle. It was getting late, but it was still daylight and there was little traffic. German army transport had learned to wait for dark before travelling on the open road.

Around six o'clock a small staff car appeared and was flagged down. There were two soldiers on the front seat, and a young *Luftwaffe* officer in the back; he said that he was not going to St Brieuc but to Loudéac. It would leave me twenty-five miles to go, so I accepted the lift.

The lieutenant spoke a bit of French, and while we went along I told him my story about the bicycle. We went through a village that had been bombed. The roads were so cut up that we had to take to the fields. Back on the road, the officer said:

'If the Allies are your friends why did they bomb this village? It's not a military target.'

'If you are our friends, why do your soldiers steal our bicycles?'

This put a stop to our conversation, and he spoke only to his driver and his batman on the front seat. What little German I knew, I had learnt in England during the evenings, and I had not had a chance to practise it much; but I knew just enough to follow their conversation. Apparently some Allied parachutists had been captured and he was going out to investigate. I was careful to appear uninterested.

We arrived in Loudéac after dark and after curfew. As I got out of the car, I turned and said to the officer in my best German:

'Gute Nacht, Herr Leutnant, und danke schön.'

You should have seen his face.

4

I had hardly gone fifty yards when I was stopped by a German patrol. The NCO in charge did not understand French, but when I showed him my travelling orders he took me to the *Standortkommandantur*.

A *Gefreite* interrogated me in French, and issued me with a sleeping pass for the local hotel. No vehicle was leaving Loudéac that night for St Brieuc. I was told to report to the *Feldgendarmerie* in the morning; a truck would be leaving for St Brieuc at ten o'clock.

At the hotel, I knocked and shouted for a solid twenty minutes. At last an upstairs window opened, and a grumpy voice asked me what I wanted. When I replied that I had a lodging ticket, I was told that I could go and sleep with the people who had given it to me, or with the cows if I preferred. Somebody, it seemed, had reported my arrival in a German vehicle.

There was nothing else for it; I found a hayfield and made myself a bed under some bushes, having first made sure that I hadn't been followed by a French Boche-hater. It was a mild night and I slept well. Twice I was woken by low flying aircraft.

I was up at eight. I had had no food since lunchtime the day before, so I was hungry. I found a café; several peasants were standing about, eating or drinking, and as I entered there were a lot of side glances and whisperings. I asked for bread and coffee, to be told that there was none, the Germans had taken it all; this in face of the fact that several of the customers had both in front of them. If it hadn't been for fear of the Germans, I am damn sure they would have run me out of town, or worse. It was a new experience for me, and I can't say I enjoyed it, although being a protégé of the Germans had certain advantages.

As I was still famished, I went to the counter where I could see four hard-boiled eggs and grabbed them before anybody could stop me. I asked for cider, but, of course, the Germans had drunk all their cider, so I had a drink of *eau non potable* from the wash-basin.

When I asked them how much I owed them, I was told that nobody had served me with anything. I put some money on the counter. The barman began wiping up the bar and brushed the note to the floor. The implacable loathing these French country people felt, and expressed, for everything connected with the Germans was, of course, merely another aspect of the courage of people like Le Cornec and Marie-Thérèse. I could feel it all round me, not only in the café, but even in the street as I made my way to the *Feldgendarmerie*.

There I was told to go and wait in a back yard where half-a-dozen *Feldgendarmes* were cleaning their weapons. Some had sten-guns, with which they did not seem very familiar; they had probably captured some containers from a parachute drop. I could have explained quite well how they worked, but restrained myself.

At about ten-thirty I was ordered into a small truck. As I went around to the other side, I saw two cat-o'-nine-tails, wet with fresh blood, hanging from the wall.

The truck took us to the Gestapo headquarters nearby. There were two cars waiting outside. Soon several burly men in civilian clothes came out; with the soldiers they lined the path from the door to one of the cars. I couldn't see much of what was going on, but it seemed that a man was being half-carried to the car.

Just as we were leaving a young Frenchman joined me in the back of the truck. We set off then; and as we picked up speed, a motorcyclist passed us and led the way. After twenty miles or so the convoy halted, and the motorcyclist went ahead to reconnoitre the road. It was a place where several maquisard attacks had taken place.

As everybody was getting out of the vehicles I did the same.

I wanted to see, if possible, who the man was that they were taking to St Brieuc. I pulled out a cigarette, and before anyone could react, I was almost at the second car and asking for a light. The rear door was open. They blocked my view at once; but not before I had had a glimpse inside. Between two of the plain-clothes thugs, was a young man, unconscious and almost naked, his head lolling, covered in blood from head to foot. He was handcuffed, and his feet were tied to the footrest.

This, I thought, might be one of the parachutists they had caught; they had certainly given him a mauling. As we started up again, I began to formulate a plan to rescue him; but I realized soon enough that it was a hopeless task. Not only would I risk getting killed to no purpose, but if I were captured the whole Shelburn network might be endangered. I had no right to take such a chance; but the sight of the tortured young man, propped up between those two bully-boys, made me see red.

The convoy stopped in the centre of St Brieuc to let me off. I was out in a hurry; in fact I was almost round the corner when the sergeant in charge called me back, and demanded my special *Ausweiss*, as I would not need it any longer. I played dumb and searched vainly through my pockets. My idea was to hang on to this bit of paper for future use, and to have it copied. However, the sergeant eventually said that if one of his men went through my pockets he might be luckier. I searched again and reluctantly handed it over.

I went straight to Louisette's place, which was our rendezvous. I retrieved the key from under a flagstone in the back yard, and let myself in. At last, I had a good wash and a hot meal. Refreshed, I sat on the doorstep with a book, and awaited the arrival of the others.

After a time they came slowly pedalling up the hill. Both of them were looking tired and worried. At the gate they stopped in their tracks and stared at me incredulously.

'How did you get here?' they almost shouted.

I could not resist answering:

'By courtesy of the *Wehrmacht*, the *Luftwaffe*, the *Feldgendarmerie* and the Gestapo.'

CHAPTER FIFTEEN

The Last of Shelburn

1

THAT same afternoon, I was due to make contact with some members of the Resistance. Neither Ray nor Louisette were known to them, so it would be dangerous for them if they showed up in my stead. The rendezvous was only twenty miles away, but I had to ride a bicycle to get there, and my boils were, if anything, even worse than when we left Paris.

The trip outwards was not bad, as it was downhill, but the return journey was agony. For half of it I was pedalling with only one foot as I could not sit on the saddle. Next day Louisette, who had been playing nurse to me, contacted a doctor whom she knew and could trust, and he gave me an injection which cleared the whole thing up in a couple of days.

Luckily my painful ride had not been wasted, as I had been able to arrange for the safe conduct of a big batch of parcels. These airmen had been cared for by a Countess on her estate near Yffiniac. The place had been visited by the Gestapo the year before, and they had arrested her husband, who had subsequently died in a German prison. She had decided to carry on his work; and I was glad to be able to relieve her of such dangerous guests.

Beside the parcels from Yffiniac, there were others in Guingamp, and we were scouring the countryside for stragglers. We picked up quite a few, and had enough for another full operation; so we went to Plouha to make ready.

I had posted a man near the woods where Campinchi was to send parcels from Paris. He was a Breton who had worked in England, and he spoke English quite well. Every day he searched, but no parcels ever came. It must have been the lack of bicycles that prevented them. Where a commando wouldn't have hesitated to foot it all the way, flying types weren't so hot on marching.

London was now using us as a ferry-boat service, and sending us all kinds of people who needed passage back to England. Some of them we had to go out and fetch ourselves, under directions from London; others made their own way. One batch came from a battalion of parachutists from the Special Task Force, who had come down in the western part of Brittany, and they proved a bit of an embarrassment. When they found that we could get them across the Channel, they had the idea that they could visit their folks whenever they felt lonely, and that we would put on an operation accordingly. We quickly disillusioned them.

Among our distinguished customers we had a General, who was no trouble at all, thanking us warmly for everything we did; and a French major who sent word that we were to fetch him by car from his maquis. We replied that he would do better to walk, as the Germans were watching the roads and searching all vehicles. This did not suit him at all; indeed, from his answer, I thought he must be sick and have urgent business with London, so I sent a horse and cart for him.

It was fifty miles each way, and when he arrived he was beside himself with the indignity of his mode of travel. I let him rave on for a time; then, instead of answering him, I turned to the driver of the cart and asked him why he had brought this lunatic in instead of shooting him. The major put his hand on my shoulder, intending to spin me round. I spun around all right and, drawing the ·45 Colt at my belt, I fired one shot at his head. I missed intentionally, though that was easier said than done, and he vanished into the bushes, never to be seen again.

By now we were getting well known among the Resistance groups, and although I regarded this as dangerous, it had one advantage. Our intelligence was first-class; and many times when London instructed us to pick up this person or that, we could reply that we had already done so. Others came out of the blue, and Ray was kept busy sending off messages to OK their passage.

2

On this occasion, however, the operation itself did not look easy. There were German patrols all round Plouha; so many, in fact, that I began to wonder whether they suspected something. But whether they did or not made no difference; the people that we had waiting were so important that we just had to get them across, even if it meant a fight; and we were quite ready to fight if necessary.

Thirty of our best men were brought out of the maquis to accompany the usual operators. On the evening before 'Bonaparte' the Germans were all over the place, and I thought it best to keep my people in one group, both to reduce the chances of an encounter, and to have a strong force if one should take place.

We were lucky, and met no patrol on our way to the beach, though all the farm dogs were barking as we went by. We could hear other dogs barking in the distance, and could almost follow the progress of the Germans from farm to farm.

Just in case they were after us, I left two men as sentries at the top of the cliff. They lay down in the minefield, with their sten-guns at the ready and a couple of grenades to hand. Ten minutes after we had gone down, a patrol of about ten Germans came along. They stopped at the edge of the minefield, which was marked off by barbed wire, and argued among themselves before turning round and going back—much to the relief of our two sentries, who had been wondering whether to attack, or wait and see.

They told us what had happened when we climbed back from the beach. We were amazed, for we had heard nothing; but on the way back we took care to use paths where we would leave no tracks they could follow.

Before we dispersed, we stopped in a field for a rest. Some of the men were eating; and when I enquired as to their source of food, they pointed to the bushes—raw snails!

The situation was changing rapidly. All our previous operations had been carried out under the cloak of secrecy; now we were working more openly, and were prepared to use force. This was due to the fact that the enemy was fully engaged on the Normandy front, and was moving all available troops there. Even the Gestapo were becoming less effective in tracking down saboteurs, for they could not rely on as many troops for large-scale raids. The *Feldgendarmerie* also had their hands full.

I was quite sure that eventually we should be cut off from the rest of France. The Allied landing had survived the June gale, and with shipping pouring men and materials across, it was only a matter of time before the Germans started to give ground. My mission was coming to an end.

London had definitely laid down that we were not to fight, take up sabotage, or seek intelligence information. London, however was a long way off, and we had no intention of sitting on our arses waiting for the arrival of Allied troops. We were still soldiers first. Ray, Le Cornec and I, therefore, held a conference. We came to the conclusion that we could give the Germans something more to worry about.

The Free French had been teaching the *Résistants* how to sabotage communications and ambush German troops, thus forcing them to stay in large bodies, and restricting their movement behind the front. The fear of being ambushed was beginning to tell on their morale.

In the Plouha region we had had some difficulty with Resistance groups who were carrying out acts of sabotage. They were likely to attract the attention of the Germans, and endanger our evacuation work; but when we asked them to stop their activities, they refused, unless we could give them a good reason. This, of course, we could not do, for security reasons. It was only when they received a pre-arranged message over the BBC that they agreed.

I had been against attacks on the Germans, as the Germans had a nasty habit of taking hostages and shooting ten of them for every German killed. But the time was not far off when we should be able to fight them almost openly, for they would be too busy to inflict reprisals.

At our conference we decided to form our own maquis. We had the money—even if it had been allotted for other purposes; we had a lot of brave people under our command; we were experienced leaders; and we had enough weapons for training, if not for attacks. Although we were well off for guns, pistols and grenades, we were short of rifles and light machine-guns; but we could see to this as we went along. With our contacts in London, it should not be too difficult to arrange to have what we needed parachuted in. We appointed Francis Baudet to organize the maquis and drum up recruits, while Le Cornec, Louisette and I continued to run 'Bonaparte'.

In the meantime, while our enemies were growing weaker, we were growing stronger. We now had no less than 150 armed men whom we could call upon if required. We were not yet ready to defy the enemy openly, however, and we still relied on stealth, as we had done in the past.

Towards the end of July, we put on another operation. Though we did not know it then, it was to be our last. We had only a few airmen, but several important officers whose presence was urgently required in England. With so few, it seemed pointless to go to all the trouble of hiding them in farmhouses until the evening of the operation; instead, they were to go directly to the *Maison d'Alphonse*, where they would stay until it was time for them to be taken to the beach.

This way of working had its own risks, but most of the parcels were army officers, who should be able to look after themselves. We armed them with sten-guns and grenades, while we gave the airmen pistols, which they could handle very well.

Le Cornec and I took the second group to the *Maison d'Alphonse*. It was around two o'clock in the morning when we left them there. We had barely gone 200 yards when we heard shots coming from the house. We turned back to find out what was going on, creeping silently through the fields at the rear where we could see over the wall without being seen.

Several German soldiers were standing in front of the open door engaged in violent argument. One was lying on the ground, apparently wounded in the leg. While we watched, the others carried him inside.

We were well-armed, and if they had stayed out of doors, there was no reason why we should not have surprised them and probably killed the lot. But we knew Jean Gicquel and his wife and baby were in the kitchen, and we didn't dare risk it. There was no sign of the parcels, and we wondered who had shot the soldier. Two of the Germans now came out, with Jean, and went to a neighbouring farm. A few minutes later they came back with a cart, in which they laid the wounded man, and departed.

If we went to the house then, the chances were that Jean or his charges would let fly at us, so we went to Marie-Thérèse's, which was close by, and where we knew Jean would look for us.

He soon appeared, and we heard what had happened. The Germans had knocked at the door, ordering him to open it. Jean did so and had started to move forward when he noticed shadows on either side of the door. He drew back quickly, and the two Germans fired at the same time, one hitting the other in the leg. It was just after this that we returned to the house. Jean added that the soldiers appeared to be the worse for drink, and that while they were in the kitchen, bandaging the wounded man, they kept pointing towards the ceiling and muttering:

'Tommy, Tommy, terrorists.'

A Tommy was a British soldier, and a terrorist was a French maquisard. Did the Germans know there were British servicemen concealed in the house, or was it merely that, seeing a ray of light from upstairs and hearing people talking, they had jumped to that conclusion? The regular ambushing of German units was undoubtedly having its effect on the nerves of the occupying forces: they were beginning to see groups of maquis terrorists everywhere.

As soon as the Germans had left, Jean sent the parcels into a wheatfield 200 yards away and told them to stay there, as the enemy was likely to come back in force. He himself had taken his wife and baby to a neighbouring farm and then come to report.

In the morning the Germans arrived early and set fire to the house. As it was built of stone, it did not burn very well, and they had to use a lot of incendiary bombs to get it going.

We moved Mme Gicquel and her baby to the home of one of our helpers, much further away, and everybody who heard of their plight brought in clothes.

Later on in the afternoon Le Cornec and I went to find our parcels. Their track through the corn was quite obvious, and in the next field we could see the grass moving, not by the wind. We did not want to be shot at, so we called out to them from a safe distance. We had brought them food and drink, and arranged to meet them later on.

The final 'Bonaparte' operation went off well, and without further trouble, of which we had had our fill. All in all, we counted ourselves lucky to have escaped without casualties; one house burnt down was the sole cost.

4

That was the end of 'Bonaparte', but Shelburn had not quite outlived its usefulness, as I shall explain in due course. But first, we had to undergo the experience of being liberated.

Liberation, when it came, appeared in the form of five American light tanks, commanded by a lieutenant, and followed by a few trucks loaded with petrol. They rattled through Plouha to the cheers of the inhabitants, and headed for Brest where the Germans were still holding out. The main body of the American troops had forked off east, in the direction of Paris.

Most of the German forces had been locked up in the Falaise sector, and the few enemy soldiers who remained in Brittany were left to the initiative of the local civilian fighters. These lacked any unified command, and there was quite a squabble over who was in charge of what.

Elderly officers put on their uniforms and tried to resume their former responsibilities, but were soon brushed aside by younger men who had been active in the Resistance, and who would not take orders from their elders just because they were of a higher rank. Rank, in fact, counted for little, as the younger ones were promoting themselves as fast as they could find gold braid.

Politics were rife, and stored-up hatreds came into the open. Most of the civilian authorities had disappeared or been thrown into jail without charge, simply under suspicion of having aided the enemy. It took a very brave policeman even to be seen in uniform; all kinds of armed men paraded through the streets and generally laid down the law; for the police lacked the power and the political backing necessary for them to perform their proper function.

With Shelburn's *raison d'être*, as I thought, over, I looked round for something useful to do. As Capitaine Léon, a Canadian from the British Intelligence Service, I had something of a reputation; and to enhance it, I wore a British uniform that had come in by parachute, and although it fitted me like a sack of potatoes, I was positively smart compared with most of the French who claimed to be in authority and had nothing more than armbands, home-made at that.

With these somewhat unofficial qualifications, I set up my HQ in St Brieuc, with the self-appointed task of clearing the district of any agents the Germans might have left behind, and helping to restore order.

The story of my efforts in this direction has no place in this book. It is enough to say here that, in company with an American Town Major who spoke not a word of French and hadn't the foggiest idea of what he was supposed to be doing, I spent my time trying to sort out the fearful vendettas that followed the four years of enemy occupation. Accusations of collaboration and treachery were accompanied by arbitrary imprisonment and cold-blooded murder, with the communists denouncing as traitors political opponents whose only crime was that of not being communist. I was able to rescue several unfortunates who had fallen foul of them in this way, and, on the other hand, establish the guilt of others who were loud in their protestations of innocence. Among the former was the printer from Châtelaudren who had been one of the key figures in our transport organization, and who had been falsely denounced by the communists.

I had one of the few serviceable motor-cars, a stock of petrol, and an office with Odette as secretary, a small staff, and a very comprehensive file on the local inhabitants. As a result, my days were full, and I quickly made a host of enemies. But in this situation, knowledge was power, and I knew too much for their comfort.

After some weeks of this hectic, lawless existence, normal municipal life was gradually re-established. A new *Préfet* was appointed; the police regained their authority; and the *Deuxième Bureau* set up shop. Although I was invited to co-operate with the French authorities, I knew they suspected me of ulterior motives; and the Americans regarded me with mistrust. They checked my credentials with London, and were relieved to find them in order. (On a point of interest, Intelligence Agents do not have numbers, whatever Ian Fleming may have led his readers to believe.)

With the resumption of normal life, there was no longer a place for me in St Brieuc; and in any case, all the signs pointed towards an Allied thrust to Paris, and I wanted to be in on it when it came. So I set off with Louisette in my civilian car along the highway reserved for Allied troops, and despite the obstructiveness of the military police, finally succeeded in reaching SHAEF Intelligence HQ. There I contacted Major Neave, whom I knew from London, and ceased, for the time being, to play the role of agent operating behind the enemy lines. It made a pleasant change—but didn't last for long.

5

All this time Campinchi, I knew, had been busy collecting parcels, but none of them had reached us in Brittany, and I was anxious to know where they were. The only way to find out was to send someone to Paris, and I reckoned that Louisette had the best chance of crossing the lines. A good-looking girl with a plausible story is always able to get her own way. The General Staff heard about the trip and requested information on the current situation in and around Paris. I briefed Louisette accordingly; and she set off on her bicycle. I sincerely hoped we would see her again!

We were now only forty miles or so from the place where I had told Campinchi to form a maquis of his evacuees. We wanted to bring them in if they were there, to avoid the danger of their being discovered by the Germans, and possibly shot up.

Around HQ was a bunch of commandos who had lost their units, and had formed a group of their own. They had scrounged civilian cars and cut the tops off level with the bottoms of the windows, retaining only the windshields. In these open cars they had mounted bren-guns on tripods, so that they had a full 360° field of fire. They had been patrolling with these vehicles and had been most successful.

There were six of them, and for the relief operation I planned to use them and their crews as escort and scout cars. What we needed now were some vehicles in which to carry the parcels; and having found some civilian buses in the suburbs of Laval, I got the army mechanics to straighten out the four best.

The idea was to slip through the enemy line on a small country road or track, and come back using another small road. We pored over the maps, picked our route, and sent out patrols to inspect it. They reported that the idea seemed feasible, and the operation was laid on.

Meanwhile, Louisette had returned safely from Paris. She had got in quite easily, as the Germans on guard did not seem to care what was happening around them; but the return journey had been rather stickier. In the end, her story about her sick grandfather had won over an amorous sergeant who spoke a bit of French, and he let her through. She brought with her a report on the situation in Paris, and the good news that Campinchi had sent about seventy airmen to the rendezvous.

I had worked on the assumption that I would lead the party, but at the last minute Major Neave put his foot down. He was afraid that if I were captured, with my record, and in my present uniform, German Security would make a meal of me; though the way he put it was:

'Don't be so damned selfish. Give somebody else a chance to get killed.'

So all I could do was wave the convoy good-bye as they roared off into the dawn, and wait, biting my nails, until they returned.

There was no firing after they had gone; apparently the few German soldiers they saw on the road, at a sort of guard post, had simply been tooted out of the way. As the Germans used any civilian vehicles they could get to run, the guards probably took them for one of their own convoys.

We had some breakfast, and then went out to meet them on the road by which they were to return. The American captain in command told us that the Germans had sited an anti-tank gun in the bushes beside the road. We told him about our convoy, and he arranged for the enemy to be kept busy as it came along. He had men with binoculars posted in the trees; the road was straight and they could see a long way along it.

Around eleven o'clock there was a yell from one of the look-outs. My stomach was up in my throat by now; I could just visualize the massacre. At first we could see only the leading bus about two miles away, travelling fast. Between it and us a German soldier was standing in the road, waving a red disc. The bus kept going; the German soldier disappeared, and the Americans started pouring in their full fire power.

As the bus came up to the enemy position, the four cut-down cars appeared, with the second bus, and opened fire on each side of the road. In a flash they were through and firing backwards at the Germans, while the Americans stepped up their own fire.

When we managed to catch up with them we found we had gathered in over 150 evacuees, for another network had also been sending them to this maquis. They were a bunch of very happy men. From their number, seventy-four were credited to Shelburn, which brought our total to 307 safely recovered from behind the enemy lines and returned to duty.

It meant that we had the second highest score of all the BIS networks, and the best security record, as we never suffered from enemy action. This operation, which I had named 'Rapière', was really the last, and it had an ironic twist to it.

Having brought our parcels safely through the German lines, could we get them to an embarkation port? Could we hell! All day and all night empty trucks passed our station to return to the coast and load up again, but not one of them would stop. They drove at about forty miles an hour at intervals of a hundred feet, and if you tried to flag them down, they did their level best to run you over. They would only stop for MPs, and the officer in charge of them told us to go and fly a kite, or get authority from his superiors. It took us all afternoon and part of the evening to get it, by which time our charges were wondering whether anybody wanted them back, and we were thinking it was really far simpler to run our own transport and ferry service behind the Germans' backs than rely on our friends and allies!

7

There was one more irony to come. After the liberation of Paris, I returned to my apartment. I was officially attached to MI5; but no less than three times the *concierge* reported to the French *gendarmerie* that an imposter who had lived there before the liberation, a black market operator, had now turned up again, claiming to be a Canadian officer. So insistent was she that, one morning, a party composed of a French *Commandant de Gendarmerie*, a British major from the MPs, a Canadian lieutenant from the Provost Marshal's department, and a British corporal and four men, all armed to the teeth, appeared on the doorstep and demanded that I identify myself.

As I was wearing French riding boots and breeches, an American army windbreaker, a German leather belt with '*Gott mit uns*' on the buckle, an American woollen shirt, a British beret adorned with a Canadian badge, and was carrying a Luger and a commando dagger, I could see that they had reason to be curious. What I did *not* have was identity papers.

I would very much like to end this story by saying that after months of giving the Gestapo the slip, I finished up being arrested by a Canadian MP; but I must be truthful and admit that it wasn't quite like that. The lieutenant more or less believed my story, and only took me to our HQ for identification.

The most difficult part of that, incidentally, was giving him my real name. I had almost forgotten it myself!

APPENDIX I

EXTRACT from a report by Major Neave, who was in charge of Room 900, in London, and responsible for the organization of operations:

'Dumais was short, articulate and determined. It will be remembered that it was he who accompanied O'Leary to the beach at Canet-Plage armed with an iron bar to deal with intruders. His forceful personality contrasted with that of the quiet, unflappable La Brosse. Although uncertain how he would handle local French Resistance groups, we had reason to think that he would, after special training in night embarkation, be able to carry out successful sea operations in Brittany.

Our judgement of both men was fulfilled and they produced magnificent results.

I was much afraid that both these valuable agents (Campinchi and Dr Le Balch) might have been compromised by Val Williams' arrest and they were told to take the utmost care. When La Brosse came on the air at the end of November, I was considerably relieved to find that Campinchi and Dr Le Balch were apparently still safe.

Not only was I considerably worried about the numbers of aircrew in Brittany and Paris who endangered those hiding them, but there was the imminent possibility of an Allied invasion in the spring. It seemed essential to evacuate as many airmen as we could in the next few months.

La Brosse established his radio set in Paris with a Monsieur Doré, the station master at the Gare Lachapelle and, as I heard later, even operated from his office.

In this way, the MTB from Dartmouth became known in London as 'the boat train'. La Brosse was courageously assisted by M Doré's daughter whom he married at the end of 1945.

Although I had suffered many reverses and disappointments in my eighteen months at Room 900, and much sorrow at the arrest of so many brave agents, I had the utmost confidence that the Shelburn operations would change our run of misfortune.

As I was now in charge of Room 900 and ultimately responsible for these plans, I seemed to be the person to go, (as conducting officer on the beach). But MI9 were strongly opposed to this. It was a rule that officers who knew full details of the structure of any branch of secret intelligence should not go into the field, in case they were captured and tortured. Langley had been reprimanded for flying as a passenger in a training Lysander by night over the Channel.

(Author's note: Few home officers were known to agents going into the field, and those who had to be known used false names.)

It was clear from later interrogation of the escapers that the organization was extremely thorough.

La Brosse was an efficient and punctual radio operator.

He made several journeys to and from Paris during this period with his set, . . . on these journeys he ran enormous risks.

On the night of the 29th (January 1944) I was unable to sleep and paced the floor of Room 900 thinking of the responsibilities that lay upon me for this operation. It was thought by many in MI9 to be 'extremely dangerous'. I kept ringing up the duty officer at Dartmouth for news. It was not until 9 a.m. next day that I heard of its complete success.

The MTB had returned with nineteen men. Thirteen were American airmen, four were RAF, and two were Frenchmen who wanted to join the Allied forces.

It was a tremendous triumph, after so many failures, and messages of congratulation came in the whole day.

A written message from Dumais said that the operation had gone 'a bit slowly' but that the security had been good. This message also referred to the activities of *'Roger le Légionnaire'* who had betrayed Pat and his organization.

Windham-Wright (Col Langley) reported that the whole operation was over within twenty-five minutes, including the landing of stores.

Owing to the curfew, the lorry had to collect the men from their hiding places in daylight. Kérambrun ran great risk of discovery, as he sometimes openly carried twenty Allied airmen in his lorry.

Shelburn's March operations proceeded with astonishing regularity, though not without danger.

I was able to report to the United States Air Force that a substantial proportion of those who baled out of their aircraft on these raids (Bremen, Ludwigshaven, Kiel and flying-bomb sites) were being returned within a month, and sometimes within a few days, of being shot down.

The effect on the prestige of MI9 was sensational, and what was known as the 'miracle' of Shelburn continued.

But the Shelburn organization had been an undisputed success, and by 30 March, 1944, 118 airmen had already returned.

Thus ended one of the most splendid exploits in which the Navy and agents of Room 900 ever took part.'

APPENDIX II

EXTRACT from a letter to the author from K. B. Woodhouse, an ex-RCAF pilot:

Mr Lucien Dumais:

As one of those who had the thrill of experiencing Operation Bonaparte on the night of 24 March 1944, first let me thank you with all my heart for what you did for me and over twenty others that unforgettable night. Words fail me when I try to tell of parachuting from my disabled Spitfire on 18 March 1944—almost into the hands of M Maurice Rendu who saw me bale out and land two and a half kilometres from a German installation and who beat them to me in his truck, by two minutes: of the pursuing German patrol stopping M Rendu's truck before we had gone one kilometre and inexplicably failing to detect me hidden under sacks in the back of the truck. Also of two other searches in the next few hours that were almost as close; of the trip by truck, train and on foot to many other homes in Beauvais, Paris and Guingamp. Then the ride in M Kérambrun's open truck to Plouha, and finally to the 'House of Alphonse' seven days later. It was something one would have to have experienced to believe. M Rendu's name and the name of his town were printed plainly on his truck and it was by this means I was able to write to him after the liberation of France. This was the beginning of a friendship and steady correspondence that has been going on for twenty-two years!

Through the RAF Escaping Society I was able to learn the identity of three other helpers: Madame Schneegans and Madame Olympe Vasseur of Paris, and Madame Francine Laurent of Guingamp. At one time I corresponded with them too, but lost contact with them some years ago. Madame Laurent, I have learned, died in 1954 and had been invested with the *Croix de Guerre* for her wartime work.

In 1962 I made a trip to France to thank personally any of my helpers I could find, and while in Paris, I had some success in retracing my escape route through the city, but was unsure of the Lycée St-Louis as being the home of 'Maurice' and 'Margaret' where I received my forged identity card and travel permits, which I still have, and left the imprint of my fingers on many others. Do you know if this Lycée was used as such a place and do you know the fate of the two fine people who lived there? Madame Vasseur told me she believed they were caught shortly after I passed through their hands and died in Auschwitz concentration camp.